Allyn & Bacon
Casebook Series
Substance Abuse

Edited by

Jerry L. Johnson
Grand Valley State University

George Grant, Jr.
Grand Valley State University

PEARSON

Boston   New York   San Francisco
Mexico City   Montreal   Toronto   London   Madrid   Munich   Paris
Hong Kong   Singapore   Tokyo   Cape Town   Sydney

*To all of those who have helped, advised, supported, criticized,
and forgiven. You know who you are.*
Jerry L. Johnson

*To my wife, Beverly, who inspires and supports me
in all my endeavors. In loving memory of my father and mother,
George and Dorothy Grant.*
George Grant, Jr.

Series Editor: *Patricia Quinlin*
Marketing Manager: *Kris Ellis-Levy*
Production Administrator: *Janet Domingo*
Compositor: *Galley Graphics*
Composition Buyer: *Linda Cox*
Manufacturing Buyer: *JoAnne Sweeney*
Cover Coordinator: *Rebecca Krzyzaniak*

For related titles and support materials, visit our online catalog at www.ablongman.com.

Copyright © 2005 Pearson Education, Inc.

Library of Congress Cataloging-in-Publication Data

Allyn & Bacon casebook series for substance abuse / [edited by] Jerry L. Johnson, George Grant, Jr.—1st ed.
   p. cm.
   Includes bibliographical references.
   ISBN 0-205-38942-2 (pbk.)
   1. Substance abuse—Treatment—Case studies. 2. Addicts—Counseling of—Case studies.
   3. Social work with narcotic addicts—Case studies. I. Title: Allyn and Bacon casebook series for substance abuse. II. Johnson, Jerry L. III. Grant, George, Jr.
   HV4998.A46 2005
   362.29—dc22

                                           2004052963

Printed in the United States of America

10 9 8 7 6 5 4 3   09 08 07

Contents

Preface

This text offers students the chance to study the work of experienced social workers practicing in various settings with substance abusing clients. As graduate and undergraduate social work educators, we (the editors) have struggled to find quality practice materials that translate well into a classroom setting. Over the years, we have used case materials from our practice careers, professionally produced audiovisuals, and tried other casebooks. While each had its advantages, we could not find a vehicle that allowed students to study the work of experienced practitioners that took students beyond the belief that practice is a technical endeavor that involves finding "correct" interventions to solve client problems.

We want our students to study and analyze how experienced practitioners think about practice and how they struggle to resolve ethical dilemmas and make treatment decisions that meet the needs of their clientele. We want students to review and challenge the work of others in a way that allows them to understand what comprises important practice decisions with real clients in real practice settings. That is, we want classroom materials that allow students entry into the minds of experienced practitioners.

Goals of the Casebook

This Casebook focuses on practice with substance abusing clients in a variety of settings and from diverse backgrounds. Our goal is to provide students with an experience that:

1. Provides personal and intimate glimpses into the thinking and actions of experienced practitioners as they work with clients. In each case, students may demonstrate their understanding of the cases and how and/or why the authors approached their case in the manner presented.

2. Provides a vehicle to evaluate the process, ideas, and methods used by the authors. We also wanted to provide students a chance to present their ideas about how they would have worked differently with the same case.

3. Affords students the opportunity to use evidence-based practice findings (Gibbs, 2003; Cournoyer, 2004) as part of the case review and planning process. We challenge students to base practice judgments and case planning exercises on current practice evidence available through library and/or electronic searches, and practice wisdom gained through consultation and personal experience when the evidence is conflicted or lacking.

To meet our goals, the cases we included in this text focus on the practice process, specifically client engagement, assessment, and the resultant clinical process, including the inevitable ethical dilemmas that consistently arise in daily practice. We aim to demonstrate the technical and artistic elements involved in developing and managing the various simultaneous processes involved in practice. While we recognize the difficulty of presenting process information (circular) in a linear medium (book), we have tried to do the best job possible toward this end.

To achieve our goals, we include three in-depth case studies in this text. In the first two case studies, authors guide students through the complete practice process, from initial contact to client termination and practice evaluation. The third and final case in this text offers an in-depth presentation of the first three therapy sessions with a client. Focusing heavily on multi-systemic client life history (see Chapter 1), students get a detailed look into the life history and presentation of the client. Then, we challenge students to "finish the case" by using client information and classroom learning to develop a written narrative assessment, diagnostic statement, treatment and intervention plan, termination and follow-up plan, and a plan to evaluate practice. We have used these cases as in-class exercises, the basis for semester-long term papers, and as comprehensive final examinations that integrate multifaceted student learning in practice courses across the curriculum.

Rationale

As former practitioners, we chose the cases carefully. Therefore, the cases in this text focus on the process (thinking, planning, and decision-making) of social work practice and not necessarily on techniques or outcome. Do not be fooled by this statement. Obviously, we believe in successful client outcome based, at least in part, on the use of evidence-based practice methods and current research findings. As important as this is, it is not our focus here with good reason. Our experience suggests that instructive process occurs in cases that have successful and unsuccessful outcome. In fact, we often learned more from unsuccessful cases than successful cases. We learned the most when events did not play out as planned. While some of the cases terminated successfully, others did not. This is not a commentary on the author or the author's skill level. Everyone has cases (sometimes too many) that do not turn out as planned. We chose cases based on one simple criterion: did it provide the best possible hope for practice education. We asked authors to teach practice by considering cases that were interesting and difficult, regardless of outcome. We did not want the Casebook to become simply a vehicle to promote practice brilliance.

Mostly, we wanted this text to differ from other casebooks, because we were unsatisfied with casebooks as teaching tools. As part of the process of planning our Casebooks, we reviewed other casebooks and discussed with our graduate and undergraduate students approaches that best facilitated learning in the classroom. We discovered that many students were also dissatisfied with a casebook approach to education, for a variety of reasons. Below, we briefly address what our students told us about casebooks in general.

1. *Linear presentation.* One of the most significant problems involves case presentation. Generally, this involves two issues: linearity and brevity. Most written case studies give students the impression that practice actually proceeds smoothly, orderly, and in a sequential manner. These cases often leave students believing or expecting that clinical decisions are made beforehand and that practice normally proceeds as planned. In other words, students often enter the field believing that casework follows an "*A, leads to B, leads to C, leads to clients living happily ever after*" approach.

Experienced practitioners know better. In over 40 years of combined social work practice in a variety of settings, we have learned often the "hard way" that the opposite is true. We rarely, if ever, had a case proceed sequentially, whether our client is an individual, couple, family, group, community, or classroom. That is, the process of engagement (including cultural competence), assessment, treatment planning, intervention, and follow-up occur in a circular manner, rooted in the client's social, physical, and cultural context, and includes consideration of the practitioner, his or her organization, and the laws and policies that affect and/or determine the boundaries of social work practice and treatment funding.

Practice evolves in discontinuous cycles over time, including time-limited treatments mandated by the managed care system. Therefore, real-life clinical practice just as in all developing human relationships seems to consistently require stops and starts, take wrong-turns, and even, in some cases, require "do-overs." While the goal of competent practice is to facilitate an orderly helping process that includes planned change (Timberlake, Farber, & Sabatino, 2002), practice, as an orderly process, is more often a goal (or a myth) than planned certainty. Given the linearity of case presentations discussed above, readers are often left without an appreciation or understanding of practice as process.

Additionally, many of the case presentation texts we reviewed provided "hard" client data and asked students to develop treatment plans based on this data. Yet, as any experienced practitioner knows, the difficulty in practice occurs during engagement and data collection. The usual case approach often overlooks this important element of practice. While a book format limits process writing, we believe that the case format we devised here brings students closer to the "real thing."

2. *Little focus on client engagement.*   As we like to remind students, there are two words in the title of our profession: social and work. In order for the "work" to be successful, students must learn to master the "social"—primarily, client engagement and relationship building. Social work practice is relationship based (Saleebey, 2002) and, from our perspective, relies more on the processes involved in relationship building and client engagement than technical intervention skills (Johnson, 2004). Successful practice is often rooted more in the ability of practitioners to develop open and trusting relationships with client(s) than on their ability to employ specific methods of intervention (Johnson, 2004).

Yet, this critically important element of practice often goes understated or ignored. Some texts even assume that engagement skills somehow exist before learning about practice. We find this true in casebooks and primary practice texts as well. When it is discussed, engagement and relationship building is presented as a technical process that also proceeds in linear fashion. Our experience with students, employees, and practitioner/trainees over the last two decades suggests that it is wrong to assume that students and/or practitioners have competent engagement or relationship building skills. From our perspective, developing a professional relationship that involves trust and openness, where clients feel safe to dialogue about the most intimate and sometimes embarrassing events in their lives, is the primary responsibility of the practitioner, and often spells the difference between positive and negative client outcome (Johnson, 2004; Miller & Rollnick, 2002; Harper & Lantz, 1996). Hence, each case presentation tries to provide a sense of this difficult and often elusive process and some of the ways that the authors overcame challenges to the culturally competent client engagement process.

Target Audience

Our target audience for this text, and the others in the series, are advanced undergraduate as well as foundation and advanced graduate students in social work and other helping disciplines. We have tested our approach with students at several different points in their education. We find that the casebooks can be used as:

- An adjunct learning tool for undergraduates preparing for or already involved in their field practicum.
- Practice education and training for foundation-level graduate students in practice theory and/or methods courses.
- An adjunct learning tool for second-year graduate students in field practicum.
- An adjunct learning tool for undergraduate and/or graduate students in any practice courses pertaining to specific populations.

While we are social work educators, we believe the casebooks will be useful in social work and other disciplines in the human services, including counseling psychology, counseling, mental health, psychology, and specialty disciplines such as marriage and family therapy, substance abuse, and mental health degree or certificate programs. Any educational or training program designed to prepare students to work with clients in a helping capacity may find the casebooks useful as a learning tool.

Structure of Cases

We organized the case studies to maximize critical thinking, the use of professional literature, evidenced-based practice knowledge, and classroom discussion in the learning process. At various points throughout each case, we comment on issues and/or dilemmas highlighted by the case. Our comments always end with a series of questions designed to focus student learning by calling on their ability to find and evaluate evidence from the professional literature and through classroom discussion. We ask students to collect evidence on different sides of an issue, evaluate that evidence, and develop a professional position that they can defend in writing and/or discussion with other students in the classroom or seminar setting.

We hope that you find the cases and our format as instructive and helpful in your courses as we have in ours. We have field-tested our format in courses at our university, finding that students respond well to the length, depth, and rigor of the case presentations. Universally, students report that the case materials were an important part of their overall learning process.

Organization of the Text

We organized this text to maximize its utility in any course. Chapter 1 provides an overview of the Advanced Multi-Systemic (AMS) practice approach. We provide this as one potential organizing tool for students to use while reading and evaluating the subsequent cases. This chapter offers students an organized and systematic framework to use when analyzing cases and/or formulating narrative assessments, treatment, and intervention plans. Our intent is to provide a helpful tool, not make a political statement about the efficacy or popularity of one practice framework versus others. In fact, we invite faculty and students to apply whatever practice framework they wish when working the cases.

In Chapter 2, author *Catherine Simmons, MSW, MEd, BCD* presents her work with **Oliver,** a member of the military service ordered into treatment over multiple issues in his life that occurred just prior to his scheduled retirement date. This case is an excellent example of what happens when clients do not reveal their "whole" story, until circumstances require it. That is, this case demonstrates the all-too-common presentation of a chemically dependent person who does not admit to substance use and abuse until treatment hits a dead-end.

In Chapter 3, *Kelly Ward, Ph.D., LCSW, CADC* presents a case that involves a young, married mother of two who discovers multiple addictions affecting her life. In a case entitled **Carrie,** Dr. Ward takes us through her client's treatment as she proceeds from the initial intake session and inpatient substance abuse treatment, through their challenging work in outpatient treatment, ending with a successful termination. Carrie involves many of the issues and dilemmas that clients and practitioners face during the substance abuse treatment process.

The final chapter, **Frank,** presents the first three sessions of Dr. Jerry L. Johnson's treatment with a Vietnam veteran in serious legal trouble. While this case is unique because of the way Frank's current life parallels his past, it is not unique in how Frank and Dr. Johnson formed a relationship in the context of a mandated referral. Dr. Johnson presents Frank's case in significant detail, including dialogue taken from their sessions, providing the foundation for students to complete the assessment, treatment planning, intervention planning and practice evaluation process from their own practice perspectives.

Acknowledgments

We would like to thank the contributors to this text, Catherine Simmons and Kelly Ward, for their willingness to allow their work to be challenged and discussed in a public venue. We would also like to thank Patricia Quinlin and her people at Allyn and Bacon for their faith in the Casebook Series and in our ability to manage fourteen manuscripts at once. Additionally, we have to thank all of our students and student assistants that served as "guinea pigs" for our case studies. Their willingness to provide honest feedback contributes mightily to this series.

Jerry L. Johnson—I want to thank my wife, Cheryl, for her support and willingness to give me the time and encouragement to write and edit. I also owe a debt of gratitude to my dear friend Hope, for being there when I need you the most.

George Grant, Jr.—I want to thank Dean Rodney Mulder and Dr. Elaine Schott for their insight, encouragement, and support during this process. I also thank Dr. Julius Franks and Professor Daniel Groce for their intellectual discourse and unwavering support.

Contributors

The Editors

Jerry L. Johnson, Ph.D., MSW is an Associate Professor in the School of Social Work at Grand Valley State University in Grand Rapids, Michigan. He received his MSW from Grand Valley State University and his Ph.D. in sociology from Western Michigan University. Johnson has been in social work for more than 20 years as a practitioner, supervisor, administrator, consultant, teacher, and trainer. He was the recipient of two Fulbright Scholarship awards to Albania in 1998–99 and 2000–01. In addition to teaching and writing, Johnson serves in various consulting capacities in countries such as Albania and Armenia. He is the author of two previous books, *Crossing Borders—Confronting History: Intercultural Adjustment in a Post-Cold*

War World (2000, Rowan and Littlefield) and *Fundamentals of Substance Abuse Practice* (2004, Wadsworth Brooks/Cole).

George Grant, Jr., Ph.D., MSW is an Associate Professor in the School of Social Work at Grand Valley State University in Grand Rapids, Michigan. Grant, Jr., also serves as the Director of Grand Valley State University's MSW Program. He received his MSW from Grand Valley State University and Ph.D. in sociology from Western Michigan University. Grant, Jr., has a long and distinguished career as practitioner, administrator, consultant, teacher, and trainer in social work, primarily in fields dedicated to Child Welfare.

Contributors

Catherine Simmons, MSW, MEd., BCD is a licensed clinical social worker with seven years' experience as both an active duty and reserve Air Force social worker running substance abuse and domestic violence treatment programs. Currently, Simmons is a Ph.D. student at the University of Texas at Arlington.

Kelly Ward, Ph.D., LCSW, CADC is an Assistant Professor at Monmouth University in West Long Beach, New Jersey. Concurrently, she is a member of a group practice called Colts Neck Consulting Group in Colts Neck, NJ. She has practiced for more than 15 years with specialization on substance abuse, particularly with adolescents and children.

Bibliography

Cournoyer, B. R. (2004). *The evidence-based social work skills book.* Boston: Allyn and Bacon.

Gibbs, L. E. (2003). *Evidence-based practice for the helping professions: A practical guide with integrated multimedia.* Pacific Grove, CA: Brooks/Cole.

Harper, K. V., & Lantz, J. (1996). *Cross-cultural practice: Social work practice with diverse populations.* Chicago: Lyceum Books.

Johnson, J. L. (2004). *Fundamentals of substance abuse practice.* Pacific Grove, CA: Brooks/Cole.

Miller, W. R., & Rollnick, S. (2002). *Motivational interviewing: Preparing people to change addictive behavior* (2nd ed.). New York: Guilford Press.

Saleebey, D. (2002). *The strengths perspective in social work practice* (3rd ed.). Boston: Allyn and Bacon.

Timberlake, E. M., Farber, M. Z., & Sabatino, C. A. (2002). *The general method of social work practice: McMahon's generalist perspective* (4th ed.). Boston: Allyn and Bacon.

1

A Multi-Systemic Approach to Practice

Jerry L. Johnson & George Grant, Jr.

This is a practice-oriented text, designed to build practice skills with individuals, families, and groups. We intend to provide you the opportunity to study the process involved in treating real cases from the caseloads of experienced practitioners. Unlike other casebooks, we include fewer cases, but provide substantially more detail in hopes of providing a realistic look into the thinking, planning, and approach of the practitioners/authors. We challenge you to study the author's thinking and methods to understand their approach and then use critical thinking skills and the knowledge you have gained in your education and practice to propose alternative ways of treating the same clients. In other words, what would your course of action be if you were the primary practitioner responsible for these cases? Our hope is that this text provides a worthwhile and rigorous experience studying real cases as they progressed in practice.

Before proceeding to the cases, we include this chapter as an introduction to the Advanced Multi-Systemic (AMS) practice perspective. We decided to present this introduction with two primary goals in mind. First, we want you to use the information contained in this chapter to help assess and analyze the cases in this text. You will have the opportunity to complete a multi-systemic assessment, diagnoses, treatment, and intervention plan for each case. This chapter will provide the theoretical and practical basis for this exercise. Second, we hope you find that AMS makes conceptualizing cases clearer in your practice environment. We do not suggest that AMS is the only way, or even the best way for every practitioner to conceptualize cases. We simply know, through experience, that AMS is an effective way to think about practice with client-systems of all sizes and configurations. While there are many approaches to practice, AMS offers an effective way to place clinical decisions in the context of client lives and experiences, making engagement and treatment productive for clients and practitioners.

Advanced Multi-Systemic (AMS) Practice

Sociological Roots

> Whether the point of interest is a great power state or a minor literary mood, a family, a prison, and a creed—these are the kinds of questions the best social analysts have asked. They are the intellectual pivots of classic studies of (person) in society—and they are the questions inevitably raised by any mind possessing the sociological imagination. For that imagination is the capacity to shift from one perspective to another— from the political to the psychological; from examination of a single family to comparative assessment of the national budgets of the world; from the theological school to the military establishment; from considerations of an oil industry to studies of contemporary poetry. It is the capacity to range from the most impersonal and remote transformations to the most intimate features of the human self—and see the relations between the two. Back of its use is always the urge to know the social and historical meaning of the individual in the society and in the period in which he (or she) has his quality and his (or her) being. (Mills, 1959, p. 7; parentheses added)

Above, sociologist C. Wright Mills provided a seminal description of the sociological imagination. As it turns out, Mills's sociological imagination is also an apt description of AMS. Mills believed that linking people's "private troubles" to "public issues" (p. 2) was the most effective way to understand people and their issues, by placing them in historical context. It forces investigators to contextualize individuals and families in the framework of the larger social, political, economic, and historical environments in which they live. Ironically, this is also the goal of social work practice (Germain & Gitterman, 1996; Longres, 2000). Going further, Mills (1959) stated:

> We have come to know that every individual lives, from one generation to the next, in some society; that he (or she) lives out a biography, and that he (or she) lives it out within some historical sequence. By the fact of his (or her) living he (or she) contributes, however minutely, to the shaping of this society and to the course of its history, even as he (or she) is made by society and by its historical push and shove. (p. 6)

Again, Mills was not speaking as a social worker. He was an influential sociologist, speaking about a method of social research. In *The Sociological Imagination,* Mills (1959) proposed this as a method to understand the links between people, their daily lives, and their multi-systemic environment. Yet, while laying the theoretical groundwork for social research, Mills also provided the theoretical foundation for an effective approach to social work practice. We find four relevant points in *The Sociological Imagination* that translate directly to social work practice.

1. It is crucial to recognize the relationships between people's personal issues and strengths (private troubles) and the issues (political, economic, social, historical, and legal) and strengths of the multi-systemic environment (public issues) in which people live daily and across their life span. A multi-systemic understanding includes recognizing and integrating issues and strengths at the micro (individual, family, extended kin, etc.), mezzo (local community), and macro (state, region, national, and international policy, laws, political, economic, and social) levels during client engagement, assessment, treatment, follow-up, and evaluation of practice.

2. This depth of understanding (by social workers and, especially, clients) can lead to change in people's lives. We speak here about second-order change, or, significant change that makes a long-term difference in people's lives; change that helps people view themselves differently in relationship to their world. This level of change becomes possible when people make multi-systemic links in a way that makes sense to them (Freire, 1993). In other words, clients become "empowered" to change when they understand their life in the context of their world, and realize that they have previously unforeseen or unimagined choices in how they live, think, believe, and act.

3. Any assessment and/or clinical diagnoses that exclude multi-systemic links do not provide a holistic picture of people's lives, their troubles, and/or strengths. In sociology, this leads to a reductionist view of people and society, while in social work it reduces the likelihood that services will be provided (or received by clients) in a way that addresses client problems and utilizes client strengths in a meaningful way. The opportunity for change is reduced whenever client life history is overlooked because it does not fit, or is not called for, in a practitioner's preferred method of helping, or because of shortcuts many people believe are needed in a managed care environment. One cannot learn too much about their clients, their lives, and their attitudes, beliefs, and values as it relates to the private troubles presented in treatment.

4. Inherent in AMS and foundational to achieving all that was discussed above relies on practitioners being able to rapidly develop rapport with clients that leads to engagement in treatment. In this text, client engagement

> . . . occurs when you develop, in collaboration with clients, a trusting and open professional relationship that promotes hope and presents viable prospects for change. Successful engagement occurs when you create a social context in which vulnerable people (who often hold jaded attitudes toward helping professionals) can share their innermost feelings, as well as their most embarrassing and shameful behavior with you, a *total stranger.* (Johnson, 2004, p. 93; emphasis in original)

AMS Overview

First, we should define two important terms that comprise AMS. Understanding these terms is important, because they provide the foundation for understanding the language and concepts used throughout the remainder of this chapter.

1. Advanced. According to Derezotes (2000), "the most advanced theory is also the most inclusive" (p. viii). AMS is advanced because it is inclusive. It requires responsible practitioners, in positions of responsibility (perhaps as solo practitioners) to acquire a depth of knowledge, skills, and self-awareness that allows for an inclusive application of knowledge acquired in the areas of human behavior in the social environment, social welfare policy, social research and practice evaluation, and multiple practice methods and approaches in service of clients and client systems of various sizes, types, and configurations.

AMS practitioners are expected to have the most inclusive preparation possible, "both the broad generalist base of knowledge, skills, and values and an in-depth proficiency in practice . . . with selected social work methods and populations" (Derezotes, 2000, p. xii). Hence, advanced practitioners are well-trained and, with in-depth knowledge, are often in positions of being responsible for clients as primary practitioners. They are afforded the responsibility for engaging, assessing, intervening, and evaluating practice, ensuring that clients are ethically treated in a way that is culturally competent and respectful of their client's worldview. In other words, AMS practitioners develop the knowledge, skills, and values needed to be leaders in their organizations, communities, the social work profession, and especially in the treatment of their clients. The remainder of this chapter explains why AMS is an advanced approach to practice.

2. Multi-Systemic. From the earliest moments in their education, social workers learn a systems perspective that emphasizes the connectedness between people and their problems to the complex interrelationships that exist in their client's world (Timberlake, Farber, & Sabatino, 2002). To explain these connections, systems theory emphasizes three important concepts: wholeness, relationships, and homeostasis. Wholeness refers to the notion that the various parts or elements (subsystem) of a system interact to form a whole that best describes the system in question. This concept asserts that no system can be understood or explained unless the connectedness of the subsystems to the whole are understood or explained. In other words, the whole is greater than the sum of its parts. Moreover, systems theory also posits that change in one subsystem will affect change in the system as a whole.

In terms of systems theory, relationship refers to the patterns of interaction and overall structures that exist within and between subsystems. The nature of these relationships is more important than the system itself. That is, when trying to understand or explain a system (individual, family, or organization, etc.), how subsystems connect through relationships, the characteristics of the relationships between subsystems, and how the subsystems interact provide clues to understanding the system as a whole. Hence, the application of systems theory is primarily based on understanding relationships. As someone once said about systems theory, in systems problems occur between people and subsystems (relationships), not "in" them. People's internal problems relate to the nature of the relationships in the systems where they live and interact.

Homeostasis refers to the notion that most living systems work to maintain and preserve the existing system, or the status quo. For example, family members often assume roles that serve to protect and maintain family stability, often at the expense of "needed" change. The same can be said for organizations or groups. The natural tendency toward homeostasis in systems represents what we call the "dilemma of change" (Johnson, 2004). This can best be described as the apparent conflict, or what appears to be client resistance or lack of motivation, that often occurs when clients approach moments of significant change. Systems of all types and configurations struggle with the dilemma of change: should they change to the unknown or remain the same, even if the status quo is unhealthy or unproductive? Put differently, systems strive for stability, even at the expense of health and well-being of individual members and/or the system itself.

What do we mean then, by the term *multi-systemic*? Clients (individuals, families, etc.) are systems that interact with a number of different systems simultaneously. These systems exist and interact at multiple levels, ranging from the micro level (individual and families), the mezzo level (local community, institutions, organizations, the practitioner and their agency, etc.), to the macro level (culture, laws and policy, politics, oppression and discrimination, international events, etc.). How these various systems come together, interact, and adapt, along with the relationships that exist within and between each system work together to comprise the "whole" that is the client, or client-system. In practice, the client (individual, couple, family, etc.) is not the "system," but one of many interacting subsystems in a maze of other subsystems constantly interacting to create the system—the client plus elements from multiple subsystems at each level. It would be a mistake to view the client as the whole system. They are but one facet of a multi-dimensional and multi-level system comprised of the client and various other subsystems at the micro, mezzo, and macro levels.

Therefore, the term *multi-systemic* refers to the nature of a system comprised of the various multi-level subsystems described above. A multi-systemic perspective recognizes that clients are *one part or subsystem* in relationship with other subsystemic influences occurring on different levels. This level of understanding—the system as the whole produced through multi-systemic subsystem interactions—is the main unit of investigation for practice. As stated above, it is narrow to consider the client as a functioning independent system with peripheral involvement with other systems existing outside of their intimate world. These issues and relationships work together to help shape and mold the client who, in turn, shapes and molds their relationship to the other subsystems. Yet, the person-of-the-client is but one part of the system in question during practice.

AMS provides an organized framework for gathering, conceptualizing, and analyzing multi-systemic client data and for proceeding with the helping process. It defines the difference between social work and other disciplines in the helping professions at the level of theory and practice. How, you ask? Unlike other professional disciplines that tend to focus on one or a few domains (i.e., psychology, medicine, etc.), AMS provides a comprehensive and holistic "picture" of clients or client-systems in the context of their environment by considering information about multiple personal and systemic domains simultaneously.

Resting on the generalist foundation taught in all Council on Social Work Education (CSWE) accredited undergraduate and foundation-level graduate programs, AMS requires practitioners to contextualize client issues in the context of the multiple interactions that occur between the client/client-system and the social, economic, legal, political, and physical environment in which the client lives. It is a unifying perspective based in the client's life, history, and culture that guides the process of collecting and analyzing client life information and intervening to promote personal choice through a comprehensive, multi-systemic framework. Beginning with culturally competent client engagement, a comprehensive multi-systemic assessment points toward a holistically based treatment plan that requires practitioners to select and utilize appropriate practice theories, models, and methods—or combinations thereof—that best fit the client's unique circumstances and needs.

AMS is not a practice theory, model, or method itself. It is a perspective or framework for conceptualizing client-systems. It relies on the practitioner's ability to use a variety of theories, models, and methods, and to incorporate knowledge from human behavior, social policy, research/evaluation, and practice into their routine approach with clients. For example, an AMS practitioner will have the skills to apply different approaches to individual treatment (client-centered, cognitive-behavioral, etc.), family treatment (structural, narrative, Bowenian, etc.), work with couples, in groups, arrange for specialized care if needed, and, as an advocate on behalf of their client. It may also require practitioners to treat clients in a multi-modal approach (i.e., individual and group treatments simultaneously).

Practitioners not only must know how to apply different approaches but also how to determine, primarily through the early engagement and assessment process, which theory, model, or approach (direct or indirect, for example) would work best for a particular client. Hence, successful practice using AMS relies heavily on the practitioner's ability to competently engage and multi-systemically assess client problems and strengths. Practitioners must simultaneously develop a sense of their client's personal interaction and relationship style—especially related to how they relate to authority figures—when determining which approach would best suit the client. For example, a reserved, quiet, or thoughtful client or someone who lacks assertiveness may not be well-served by a directive, confrontational approach, regardless of the practitioner's preference. Moreover, AMS practitioners rely on professional practice research and outcome studies to help determine which approach or intervention package might work best for particular clients and/or client-systems. AMS expects practitioners to know how to find and evaluate practice research in their practice areas or specialties.

Elements of the Advanced Multi-Systemic Approach to Social Work Practice

The advanced multi-systemic approach entails the following seven distinct, yet integrated elements of theory and practice. Each is explained below.

Ecological Systems Perspective

One important subcategory of systems therapy for social work is the ecological systems perspective. This perspective combines important concepts from the science of ecology and general systems theory into a way of viewing client problems and strengths in social work practice. In recent years, it has become the prevailing perspective for social work practice (Miley, O'Melia, & DuBois, 2004). The ecological systems perspective—sometimes referred to as the ecosystems perspective—is a useful metaphor for guiding social workers as they think about cases (Germain & Gitterman, 1980).

Ecology focuses on how subsystems work together and adapt. In ecology, adaptation is "a dynamic process between people and their environments as people grow, achieve competence, and make contributions to others" (Greif, 1986, p. 225). Insight from ecology leads to an analysis of how people fit within their environment and what adaptations are made in the fit between people and their environments. Problems develop as a function of inadequate or improper adaptation or fit between people and their environments.

General systems theory focuses on how human systems interact. It focuses specifically on how people grow, survive, change, and achieve stability or instability in the complex world of multiple systemic interactions (Miley, O'Melia, & DuBois, 2004). General systems theory has contributed significantly to the growth of the family therapy field and to how social workers understand their clients.

Together, ecology and general systems theory evolved into what social workers know as the ecological systems perspective. The ecological systems perspective provides a systemic framework for understanding the many ways that persons and environments interact. Accordingly, individuals and their individual circumstances can be understood in the context of these interactions. The ecological systems perspective provides an important part of the foundation for AMS. Miley, O'Melia, and DuBois (2004) provide an excellent summary of the ecological systems perspective. They suggest that it,

1. Presents a dynamic view of human beings as system interactions in context.
2. Emphasizes the significance of human system interactions.
3. Traces how human behavior and interaction develop over time in response to internal and external forces.
4. Describes current behavior as an adaptive fit of "persons in situations."
5. Conceptualizes all interaction as adaptive or logical in context.
6. Reveals multiple options for change within persons, their social groups, and in their social and physical environments (p. 33).

Social Constructionism

To maintain AMS as an inclusive practice approach, we need to build on the ecological systems perspective by including ideas derived from social constructionism. Social constructionism builds on the ecological systems perspective by introducing ideas about how people define themselves and their environment. Social constructionism also, by definition, introduces the role of culture in the meaning people give to themselves and other systems in their multi-systemic environments. The ecological systems perspective discusses relationships at the systemic level. Social constructionism introduces meaning and value into the equation, allowing for a deeper understanding and appreciation of the nature of multi-systemic relationships and adaptations.

Usually, people assume that reality is something "out there" that hits them in the face, something that independently exists, and people must learn to "deal with it." Social constructionism posits something different. Evolving as a critique of the "one reality" belief system, social constructionism points out that the world is comprised of multiple realities. People define their own reality and then live within those definitions. Accordingly, the definition of reality will be different for everyone. Hence, social constructionism deals primarily with meaning, or the systemic processes by which people come to define themselves in their social world. As sociologist W. I. Thomas said, in what has become known as the Thomas Theorem, "If people define situations as real, they are real in their consequences."

For example, some people believe that they can influence the way computerized slot machines pay out winnings by the way they sit, the feeling they get from the machine as they look at it in the casino, by the clothes they are wearing, or by how they trigger the machine, either by pushing the button or pulling the handle. Likewise, many athletes believe that a particular article of clothing, a routine for getting dressed, and/or a certain pregame meal dictates the quality of their athletic prowess that day.

Illogical to most people, the belief that they can influence a computerized machine, that the machine emits feelings, or that an article of clothing dictates athletic prowess is real to some people. For these people, their beliefs influence the way they live. Perhaps you have ideas or "superstitions" that you believe influence how your life goes on a particular day. This is a common occurrence. These people are not necessarily out of touch with objective reality. While people may know, at some level, that slot machines pay out winnings according to preset, computerized odds or that athletic prowess has nothing to do with dressing routines, the belief systems continue. What dictates the behavior and beliefs discussed above or in daily "super-stitions" have nothing to do with objective reality and everything to do with people's subjective reality. Subjective reality—or a person's learned definition of the situation—overrides objectivity and helps determine how people behave and/or what they believe.

While these examples may be simplistic, according to social constructionism, the same processes influence everyone—always. In practice, understanding that people's behavior does not depend on the objective existence of something, but on their subjective interpretation of it, is crucial to effective application of AMS. This knowledge is most helpful during client engagement. If practitioners remember that practice is about understanding people's perceptions and not objective reality, they reduce the likelihood that clients will feel misunderstood, there will be fewer dis-agreements, and it becomes easier to avoid the trap of defining normal behavior as client resistance or a diagnosable mental disorder. This perspective contributes to a professional relationship based in the client's life and belief systems, is consistent with his or her worldview, and one that is culturally appropriate for the client. Being mindful that the definitions people learn from their culture underlies not only what they do but also what they perceive, feel, and think places practitioners on the cor-rect path to "start where the client is." Social constructionism emphasizes the cul-tural uniqueness of each client and/or client-system and the need to understand each client and/or client-system in her own context and belief systems, not the practi-tioner's context or belief systems.

Social constructionism also posits that different people attribute different meaning to the same events, because the interactional contexts and the way individ-uals interpret these contexts are different for everyone, even within the same fami-ly or community. One cannot assume that people raised in the same family will define their social world similarly. Individuals, in the context of their environments, derive meaning through a complex process of individual interpretation. This is how siblings from the same family can be so different, almost as if they did not grow up in the same family. For example, the sound of gunfire in the middle of the night may be frightening or normal, depending upon where a person resides and what is routine and accepted in his specific environment. Moreover, simply because some members of a family or community understand nightly gun-fire as normal does not mean that others in the same family or community will feel the same.

Additionally, social constructionism examines how people construct meaning with language and established or evolving cultural beliefs. For example, alcohol consumption is defined as problematic depending upon how the concept of "alcohol problem" is socially constructed in specific environments. Clients from so-called drinking cultures may define drinking six alcoholic drinks daily as normal, while someone from a different cultural background may see this level of consumption as problematic. One of the authors worked in Russia and found an issue that demonstrates this point explicitly. Colleagues in Russia stated rather emphatically that consuming one "bottle" (approximately a U.S. pint) of vodka per day was acceptable and normal. People that consume more than one bottle per day were defined as having a drinking problem. The same level of consumption in the United States would be considered by most as clear evidence of problem drinking.

Biopsychosocial Perspective

Alone, the ecological systems perspective, even with the addition of social constructionism, does not provide the basis for the holistic understanding required by AMS. While it provides a multi-systemic lens, the ecological systems perspective focuses mostly on externals. That is, how people interact and adapt to their environments and how environments interact and adapt to people. Yet, much of what practitioners consider "clinical" focuses on "internals" or human psychological and emotional functioning. Therefore, the ecological systems perspective provides only one part of the holistic picture required by the advanced multi-systemic approach. By adding the biopsychosocial perspective, practitioners can consider the internal workings of human beings to help explain how external and internal subsystems interact.

What is the biopsychosocial perspective? It is a theoretical perspective that considers how human biological, psychological, and social-functioning subsystems interact to account for how people live in their environment. Similar to social systems, human beings are also multidimensional systems comprised of multiple subsystems constantly interacting in their environment, the human body. The biopsychosocial perspective applies multi-systemic thinking to individual human beings.

Several elements comprise the biopsychosocial perspective. Longres (2000) identifies two dimensions of individual functioning, the biophysical and the psychological; subdividing the psychological into three subdimensions: the cognitive, affective, and behavioral. Elsewhere, we added the spiritual/existential dimension to this conception (Johnson, 2004). Understanding how the biological, psychological, spiritual and existential, and social subsystems interact is instrumental in developing an appreciation of how individuals influence and are influenced by their social systemic environments. Realizing that each of these dimensions interacts with external social and environmental systems allow practitioners to enlarge their frame of reference, leading to a more holistic multi-systemic view of clients and client-systems.

Strengths/Empowerment Perspective

Over the last few years, the strengths perspective has emerged as an important part of social work theory and practice. The strengths perspective represents a significant change in how social workers conceptualize clients and client-systems. According to Saleebey (2002), it is "a versatile practice approach, relying heavily on ingenuity and creativity. . . . Rather than focusing on problems, your eye turns toward possibility" (p. 1). Strengths-based practitioners believe in the power of possibility and hope in helping people overcome problems by focusing on, locating, and supporting existing personal or systemic strengths and resiliencies. The strengths perspective is based on the belief that people, regardless of the severity of their problems, have the capabilities and resources to play an active role in helping solve their own problems. The practitioner's role is to engage clients in a way that unleashes these capabilities and resources toward solving problems and changing lives.

Empowerment

Any discussion of strengths-based approaches must also consider empowerment as an instrumental element of the approach. Empowerment, as a term in social work, has evolved over the years. We choose a definition of empowerment that focuses on power; internal, interpersonal, and environmental (Parsons, Gutierrez, & Cox, 1998). According to Parsons, Gutierrez, and Cox (1998),

> In its most positive sense, power is (1) the ability to influence the course of one's life, (2) an expression of self worth, (3) the capacity to work with others to control aspects of public life, and (4) access to the mechanisms of public decision making. When used negatively, though, it can also block opportunities for stigmatized groups, exclude others and their concerns from decision making, and be a way to control others. (p. 8)

Hence, empowerment in practice is a process (Parsons, Gutierrez, and Cox, 1998) firmly grounded in ecological systems and strength-based approaches that focus on gaining power by individuals, families, groups, organizations, or communities. It is based on two related assumptions: (1) all human beings are potentially competent, even in extremely challenging situations, and (2) all human beings are subject to various degrees of powerlessness (Cox & Parsons, 1994, p. 17) and oppression (Freire, 1993). People internalize their sense of powerlessness and oppression in a way that their definition of self in the world is limited, often eliminating any notion that they can act in their own behalf in a positive manner.

An empowerment approach makes practical connections between power and powerlessness. It illuminates how these factors interact to influence clients in their daily life. Empowerment is not achieved through a single intervention, nor is it something that can be "done" to another. Empowerment does not occur through neglect or by simply giving responsibility for life and well-being to the poor or troubled, allowing them to be "free" from government regulation, support, or professional assistance. In other words, empowerment of disenfranchised groups does not occur simply by dismantling systems (such as the welfare system) to allow these groups or individuals to take responsibility for themselves. Hence, empowerment does not preclude helping.

Consistent with our definition, empowerment develops through the approach taken toward helping, not the act of helping itself. Empowerment is a sense of gained or regained power that someone attains in their life that provides the foundation for change in the short term, and stimulates belief in their ability to positively influence their lives over the long term. Empowerment occurs as a function of the long-term approach of the practitioner and the professional relationship developed between practitioner and client. One cannot provide an empowering context through a constant focus on problems, deficits, inadequacies, negative labeling, and dependency.

The Power of Choice

Choice is an instrumental part of strengths-based and empowerment approaches, by recognizing that people, because of inherent strengths and capabilities, can make informed choices about their lives, just like people who are not clients. Practitioners work toward offering people choices about how they define their lives and problems, the extent to which they want to address their problems, and the means or mechanisms through which change should occur. Clients become active and instrumental partners in the helping process. They are not passive vessels, waiting for practitioners to "change them" through some crafty intervention or technique.

We are not talking about the false choices sometimes given to clients by practitioners. For example, clients with substance abuse problems are often told that they must either abstain or leave treatment. Most practitioners ignore or use as evidence of denial, client requests to attempt so-called controlled use. If practitioners were interested in offering true choice, they would work with these clients toward their controlled-drinking goal in an effort to reduce the potential harm that may result from their use of substances (Johnson, 2004; van Wormer & Davis, 2003), even if the practitioner believes that controlled drinking is not possible. Abstinence would become the goal only when their clients choose to include it as a goal.

Client Engagement as Cultural Competence

Empowerment (choice) occurs through a process of culturally competent client engagement, created by identifying strengths, generating dialogue targeted at revealing the extent of people's oppression (Freire, 1993) and respecting their right to make informed choices in their lives. Accordingly, empowerment is the "transformation from individual and collective powerlessness to personal, political, and cultural power" (GlenMaye, 1998, p. 29), through a strengths-based relationship with a professional helper.

Successful application of AMS requires the ability to engage clients in open and trusting professional relationships. The skills needed to engage clients from different backgrounds and with different personal and cultural histories are what drives practice; what determines the difference between successful and unsuccessful practice. Advanced client engagement skills allow the practitioner to elicit in-depth, multi-systemic information in a dialogue between client and practitioner (Johnson, 2004), providing the foundation for strengths-based client empowerment leading to change.

Earlier, we defined client engagement as a mutual process occurring between clients and practitioners in a professional context, created by practitioners. In other words, creating the professional space and open atmosphere that allows engagement to flourish is the primary responsibility of the practitioner, not the client. Practitioners must have the skills and knowledge to adjust their approach toward specific clients and the client's cultural context and not *vice versa*. Clients do not adjust to us and our beliefs, values, and practices—we adjust to them. When that occurs, the foundation exists for client engagement. By definition, relationships of this nature must be performed in a culturally competent manner. Yet, what does this mean?

Over the last two decades, social work and other helping professions have been concerned with cultural competence in practice (Fong, 2001). Beginning in the late 1970s, the professional literature has been replete with ideas, definitions, and practice models designed to increase cultural awareness and promote culturally appropriate practice methods. Yet, despite the attention given to the issue, there remains confusion about how to define and teach culturally competent practice.

Structural and Historical Systems of Oppression: Who Holds the Power?

Often embedded in laws, policies, and social institutions are oppressive influences such as racism, sexism, homophobia, and classism, to name a few. These structural issues play a significant role in the lives of clients (through maltreatment and discrimination) and in social work practice. How people are treated (or how they internalize historical treatment of self, family, friends, and/or ancestors) shapes how they believe, think, and act in the present. Oppression affects how they perceive that others feel about them, how they view the world and their place in it, and how receptive they are to professional service providers. Therefore, culturally competent practice must consider the impact of structural systems of oppression and injustice on clients, their problems, strengths, and potential for change.

Oppression is a by-product of socially constructed notions of power, privilege, control, and hierarchies of difference. As stated above, it is created and maintained by differences in power. By definition, those who have power can force people to abide by the rules, standards, and actions the powerful deem worthwhile, mandatory, or acceptable. Those who hold power can enforce particular worldviews; deny equal access and opportunity to housing, employment, or health care; define right and wrong, normal and abnormal; and imprison, confine, and/or commit physical, emotional, or mental violence against the powerless (McLaren, 1995; Freire, 1993). Most importantly, power permits the holder to "set the very terms of power" (Appleby, 2001, p. 37). It defines the interaction between the oppressed and the oppressor, and between the social worker and client.

Social institutions and practices are developed and maintained by the dominant culture to meet *its* needs and maintain *its* power. Everything and everybody is judged and classified accordingly. Even when the majority culture develops programs or engages in helping activities, these efforts will not include measures that threaten the dominant group's position at the top of the social hierarchy (Freire, 1993). For example, Kozol (1991) wrote eloquently about how public schools fail by design, while Freire (1993) wrote about how state welfare and private charity provide short-term assistance while ensuring that there are not enough resources to lift people permanently out of poverty.

Oppression is neither an academic nor a theoretical consideration; it is not a faded relic of a bygone era. Racism did not end with the civil rights movement, and sexism was not eradicated by the feminist movement. Understanding how systems of oppression work in people's lives is of paramount importance for every individual and family seeking professional help, including those who belong to the *same* race, gender, and class as the practitioner. No two individuals, regardless of their personal demographics, experience the world in the same way. Often, clients are treated ineffectively by professional helpers who mistakenly believe that people who look or act the same will experience the world in similar ways. These workers base their assumptions about clients on stereotypic descriptions of culture, lifestyle, beliefs, and practices. They take group-level data (i.e., many African American adolescents join gangs because of broken families and poverty) and assume that *all* African American teenagers are gang members from single-parent families. Social work values and ethics demand a higher standard, one that compels us to go beyond stereotypes. Our job is to discover, understand, and utilize personal differences in the assessment and treatment process to benefit clients, not use differences as a way of limiting clients' potential for health and well-being.

We cannot accurately assess or treat people without considering the effects of oppression related to race, ethnicity, culture, sexual preference, gender, or physical/emotional status. We need to understand how oppression influences our clients' beliefs about problems and potential approaches to problem solving, and how it determines what kind of support they can expect to receive if they decide to seek help. For example, despite the widely held belief that chemical dependency is an equal opportunity disease (Gordon, 1993), it is clear that some people are more vulnerable than others. While some of the general themes of chemical dependency may appear universal, each client is unique. That is, an individual's dependency results from personal behavior, culture (including the history of one's culture), past experiences, and family interacting with larger social systems that provide opportunities or impose limits on the individual (Johnson, 2000).

Systems of oppression ensure unequal access to resources for certain individuals, families, and communities. However, while all oppressed people are similar in that they lack the power to define their place in the social hierarchy, oppression based on race, gender, sexual orientation, class, and other social factors is expressed in a variety of ways. Learning about cultural nuances is important in client assessment, treatment planning, and treatment (Lum, 1999). According to Pinderhughes (1989), there is no such thing as culture-free service delivery. Cultural differences between clients and social workers in terms of values, norms, beliefs, attitudes, lifestyles, and life opportunities affect every aspect of practice.

What Is Culture?

Many different concepts of culture are used in social work, sociology, and anthropology. Smelser (1992) considers culture a "system of patterned values, meanings, and beliefs that give cognitive structure to the world, provide a basis for coordinating and controlling human interactions, and constitute a link as the system is transmitted from one generation to another" (p. 11). Geertz (1973) regarded culture as simultaneously a product of and a guide to people searching for organized categories and interpretations that provide a meaningful experiential link to their social life. Building upon these two ideas, in this book we abide by the following definition of culture proposed elsewhere (Johnson, 2000):

> Culture is historical, bound up in traditions and practices passed through generations; memories of events—real or imagined—that define a people and their worldview. (Culture) is viewed as collective subjectivity, or a way of life adopted by a community that ultimately defines their worldview. (p. 121)

Consistent with this definition, the collective subjectivities called culture are pervasive forces in the way people interact, believe, think, feel, and act in their social world. Culture plays a significant role in shaping how people view the world. As a historical force, in part built on ideas, definitions, and events passed through generations, culture also defines people's level of social acceptance by the wider community; shapes how people live, think, and act; and influences how people perceive that others feel about them and how they view the world and their place in it. Thus, it is impossible to understand a client without grasping their cultural foundations.

Cultural Competence

As stated earlier, over the years many different ideas and definitions of what constitutes culturally competent practice have developed, as indicated by the growth of the professional literature since the late 1970s. To date, focus has primarily been placed in two areas: (1) the need for practitioners to be aware or their own cultural beliefs, ideas, and identities leading to cultural sensitivity, and (2) learning factual and descriptive information about various ethnic and racial groups based mostly on group-level survey data and analyses. Fong (2001) suggests that culture is often considered "tangential" to individual functioning and not central to the client's functioning (p. 5).

To address this issue, Fong (2001) builds on Lum's (1999) culturally competent practice model that focuses on four areas: (1) cultural awareness, (2) knowledge acquisition, (3) skill development, and (4) inductive learning. Besides inductive learning, Lum's model places focuses mainly on practitioners in perpetual self-awareness, gaining knowledge about cultures, and skill building. While these are important ideas for cultural competence, Fong (2001) calls for a shift in thinking and practice, "to provide a culturally competent service focused solely on the client rather than the social worker and what he or she brings to the awareness of ethnicity" (p. 5). Fong (2001) suggests an "extension" (p. 6) of Lum's model by turning the focus of each of the four elements away from the practitioner toward the client. For example, cultural awareness changes from a practitioner focus to "the social worker's understanding and the identification of the critical cultural values important to the client system and to themselves" (p. 6). This change allows Fong (2001) to remain consistent with the stated definition of culturally competent practice, insisting that practitioners

> . . . operating from an empowerment, strengths, and ecological framework, provide services, conduct assessments, and implement interventions that are reflective of the clients' cultural values and norms, congruent with their natural help-seeking behaviors, and inclusive of existing indigenous solutions. (p. 1)

While we agree with the idea that "to be culturally competent is to know the cultural values of the client-system and to use them in planning and implementing services" (Fong, 2001, p. 6), we want to make this shift the main point of a culturally competent model of client engagement. That is, beyond what should or must occur, we believe that professional education and training must focus on the skills of culturally competent client engagement that are necessary to make this happen; a model that places individual client cultural information at the center of practice. We agree with Fong (2001) that having culturally sensitive or culturally aware practitioners is not nearly enough. Practitioner self-awareness and knowledge of different cultures does not constitute cultural competence. We strive to find a method for reaching this worthy goal.

The central issue revolves around practitioners participating in inductive learning and the skills of grounded theory. In other words, regardless of practitioner beliefs, awarenesses, or sensitivities, their job is to learn about and understand their client's world, and "ground" their theory of practice in the cultural context of their client. They develop a unique theory of human behavior in a multi-systemic context for every client. Culturally competent client engagement does not happen by assessing the extent to which client lives "fit" within existing theory and knowledge about reality, most of which is middle-class and Eurocentric at its core. Cultural competence (Johnson, 2004)

> . . . *begins* with learning about different cultures, races, personal circumstances, and structural mechanisms of oppression. It *occurs* when practitioners master the interpersonal skills needed to move beyond general descriptions of a specific culture or race to learn specific individual, family, group, or community interpretations of culture, ethnicity, and race. The culturally competent practitioner knows that within each culture are individually interpreted and practiced thoughts, beliefs, and behaviors that may or may not be consistent with group-level information. That is, there is tremendous diversity within groups, as well as between them. Individuals are unique unto

themselves, not simply interchangeable members of a specific culture, ethnicity, or race who naturally abide by the group-level norms often taught in graduate and undergraduate courses on human diversity. (p. 105)

Culturally competent client engagement revolves around the practitioner's ability to create a relationship, through the professional use of self, based in true dialogue (Freire, 1993; Johnson, 2004). We define dialogue as "a joint endeavor, developed between people (in this case, practitioner and client) that move clients from their current state of hopelessness to a more hopeful, motivated position in their world" (Johnson, 2004, p. 97). Elsewhere (Johnson, 2004), we detailed a model of culturally competent engagement based on Freire's (1993) definitions of oppression, communication, dialogue, practitioner self-work, and the ability to exhibit worldview respect, hope, humility, trust, and empathy.

To investigate culture in a competent manner is to take a comprehensive look into people's worldview—to discover what they believe about the world and their place in it. It goes beyond race and ethnicity (although these are important issues) into how culture determines thoughts, feelings, and behaviors in daily life. This includes what culture says about people's problems; culturally appropriate strengths and resources; the impact of gender on these issues; and what it means to seek professional help (Leigh, 1998).

The larger questions to be answered are how clients uniquely and individually interpret their culture; how their beliefs, attitudes, and behaviors are shaped by that interpretation, and how these cultural beliefs and practices affect daily life and determine lifestyle in the context of the larger community. Additionally, based on their cultural membership, beliefs, and practices, practitioners need to discover the potential and real barriers faced by clients in the world. Many clients, because they are part of non-majority cultures, face issues generated by social systems of oppression such as racism, sexism, homophobia, and ethnocentrism that expose them to limitations and barriers that others do not face.

What is the value of culturally competent client engagement? Helping clients discuss their attitudes, beliefs, and behaviors in the context of their culture—including their religious or spiritual belief systems—offers valuable information about their worldview, sense of social and spiritual connection, and/or practical involvement in their social world. Moreover, establishing connections between their unique interpretation of their culture and their daily life provides vital clues about people's belief systems, attitudes, expectations (social construction of reality), and explanation of behaviors that cannot be understood outside the context of their socially constructed interpretation of culture.

A Cautionary Note

It is easy to remember to ask about culture when clients are obviously different (i.e., different races, countries of origin, etc.). However, many practitioners forgo cultural investigation with clients they consider to have the same cultural background as the practitioner. For example, the search for differences between European-Americans with Christian beliefs—if the social worker shares these characteristics—gets lost in mutual assumptions, based on the misguided belief that there are no important differences between them. The same is often true when clients and practitioners come from the same racial, cultural, or lifestyle backgrounds (i.e., African American practitioner and client, gay practitioner and gay client, etc.). Culturally competent practice means that practitioners are always interested in people's individual interpretation of their culture and their subjective definitions of reality, whether potential differences are readily apparent or not. Practitioners must be diligent to explore culture with clients who appear to be from the same background as the practitioner, just as they would with people who are obviously from different cultural, racial, ethnic, or religious backgrounds.

Multiple Theories & Methods

No single theory, model, or method is best suited to meet the needs of all clients (Miley, O'Melia, & DuBois, 2004). Consistent with this statement, one of the hallmarks of AMS is the expectation that practitioners must determine which theory, model, or method will best suit a particular client. Choosing from a range of approaches and interventions, AMS practitioners develop the skills and abilities to: (1) determine, based on the client's life, history, culture, and style, which treatment approach (theory and/or method) would best suit their needs and achieve the desired outcome, (2) determine which modality or modalities (individual, family, group treatment, etc.) will best meet the need of their clients, and (3) conduct treatment according to their informed clinical decisions.

Over the last 20 years or so, graduate social work education has trended toward practice specialization through concentration-based curricula. Many graduate schools of social work build on the generalist foundation by insisting that students focus on learning specific practice models or theories (disease, cognitive-behavioral, psychoanalysis, etc.) and/or specific practice methods (individual, family, group, etc.), often at the exclusion of other methods or models. For example, students often enter the field intent on doing therapy with individuals say, from a cognitive-behavioral approach only.

This trend encourages practitioners to believe that one approach or theory best represents the "Truth." Truth, in this sense, is the belief that one theory or approach works best for most people, most of the time. It helps create a practice scenario that leads practitioners to use their chosen approach with every client they treat. Therefore, practice becomes a process of the practitioner forcing clients to adjust to the practitioner's beliefs and expectations about the nature of problems, the course of treatment, and definition of positive versus negative outcomes. From this perspective, what is best for clients is determined by what the practitioner believes is best, not what clients believe is in their best interest.

Some practitioners take their belief in the Truth of a particular theory or method to extremes. They believe that one model or theory works best for all people, all the time. We found this to be common in the family therapy field, whereby some true believers insist that everyone needs family therapy—so that is all they offer. What's worse is that many of these same practitioners know and use only one particular family therapy theory and model. The "true believer" approach can cause problems, especially for clients. For example, when clients do not respond to treatment, instead of looking to other approaches, true believers simply prescribe more of the method that did not work in the first place. If a more intensive application of the method does not work, then the client's "lack of readiness" for treatment, resistance, or denial becomes the culprit. These practitioners usually give little thought to their practice approach or personal style and its impact on client "readiness" for treatment. They fail to examine the role their personal style, beliefs, attitudes, and practices have in creating the context that led to clients not succeeding in treatment.

Each practice theory and model has a relatively unique way of defining client problems, practitioner method and approach, interventions, and what constitutes successful outcome. For practitioners to believe that one theory or model is true, even if only for most people, they must believe in the universality of problems, methods and approaches, interventions, and successful outcome criteria. This contradicts the definition of theory. While being far from a concrete representation of the truth, a theory is a set of myths, expectations, guesses, and conjectures about what might be true (Best & Kellner, 1991). A theory is hypothetical; a set of ideas and explanations that need proving. No single theory can explain everything. According to Popper (1994), a theory ". . . always remains guesswork, and there is no theory that is not beset with problems" (p. 157). As such, treatment specialization can—although not always—encourage people to believe they have found the Truth where little truth exists.

Practitioners using an AMS perspective come to believe that some element of every established practice model, method, or theory may be helpful. Accordingly, every model, method, or theory can be adapted and used in a multi-systemic practice framework. As an AMS practitioner, one neither accepts any single model fully, nor disregards a model entirely if there is potential for helping a client succeed in a way that is compatible with professional social work values and ethics. These practitioners hone their critical thinking skills (Gambrill, 1997, 1990) and apply them in practice, particularly as it pertains to treatment theories, models, and methods. In the context of evidence-based practice (Cournoyer, 2004; Gibbs, 2003), sharpened critical thinking skills allow practitioners to closely read and evaluate practice theories, research, or case reports to recognize the strengths, weakness, and contradictions in theories, models, and/or policy related to social work practice.

Informed Eclecticism

The goal of AMS is for practitioners to develop an approach we call *informed eclecticism*. Informed eclecticism allows the use of multiple methods, interventions, and approaches in the context of practice that: (1) is held together by a perspective or approach that provides consistency, that makes practice choices in a way that makes sense in a particular client's life; and (2) is based, whenever possible, on the latest evidence about its efficacy with particular problems and particular clients. While it is often best to rely on empirical evidence, this data is in its infancy. AMS does not preclude the use of informed practice wisdom and personal creativity in developing intervention plans and approaches. It is up to practitioners to ensure that any treatment based in practice wisdom or that is creatively generated be discussed with colleagues, supervisors, or consultants to ensure theoretical consistency and that it fits within the code of professional ethics.

Informed eclecticism is different from the routine definition of eclecticism—the use of whatever theory, model, or method works best for their clients. While this is the goal of AMS practice specifically and social work practice in general (Timberlake, Farber, & Sabatino, 2004), it is an elusive goal indeed. Informed eclecticism often gets lost in a practitioner's quest to find something that "works." According to Gambrill (1997), eclecticism is "the view that we should adopt whatever theories or methodologies is useful in inquiry, no matter what their source and without worry about their consistency" (p. 93). The most important word in Gambrill's statement is "consistency." While there are practitioners who have managed to develop a consistent, organized, and holistic version of informed eclecticism, this is not the norm.

Too often, uninformed eclecticism resembles the following. A practitioner specializes by modality (individual therapy) and uses a variety of modality-specific ideas and practices in their work with clients; changing ideas and tactics when the approach they normally use does not "work." This often leaves the practitioner searching (mostly in vain) for the magic intervention—what "works." Moreover, while uninformed eclectic practitioners use interventions from various "schools," they remain primarily wedded to one modality. Hence, they end up confusing themselves and their clients as they search for the "right" approach, rarely looking beyond their chosen modality, and therefore, never actually looking outside of their self-imposed, theoretical cage.

For example, an uninformed eclectic practitioner specializing in individual therapy may try a cognitive approach, a client-centered approach, a Freudian approach, or a behavioral approach. A family therapy specialist may use a structural, strategic, or solution-focused approach. However, in the end, little changes. These practitioners still believe that their clients need individual or family treatment. They rarely consider potentially useful ideas and tactics taken from different modalities that could be used instead of, or in combination with, an individual or family approach, mostly because they base treatment decisions on their chosen modality.

While informed eclecticism is the goal, most find it difficult to find consistency when trying to work from a variety of models at the same time. The informed eclectic practitioners, through experience and empirical evidence, have a unifying approach that serves as the basis for using different models or methods. What is important, according to clinical outcome research, is the consistency of approach in helping facilitate successful client outcome (Gaston, 1990; Miller & Rollnick, 2002; Harper & Lantz, 1996). Trying to be eclectic makes consistency (and treatment success), quite difficult.

What uninformed eclecticism lacks is the framework needed to gain a holistic and comprehensive understanding of the client in the context of his or her life, history, and multiple environments that leads naturally to culturally consistent treatment and intervention decisions. AMS, as it is described here, provides such a framework. It is holistic, integrative, ecological, and based in the latest empirical evidence. It is an inclusive framework that bases treatment decisions on a multi-systemic assessment of specific client history and culture. It is designed, whenever possible, to capitalize on client strengths, be consistent with culturally specific help-seeking behavior, and utilize existing or formulated community-based and/or natural support systems in the client's environment.

Defining Multi-Systemic Client Information

In this section we specifically discuss the different dimensions that comprise AMS practice. This is a general look at what constitutes multi-systemic client life information. There are six levels of information that, when integrated into a life history of clients, demonstrates how multiple theories, models, and approaches can be applied to better understand, assess, and treat clients or client-systems. Generally, the six dimensions (biological, psychological, family, religious/spiritual/existential, social/environmental, and macro) encompass range of information needed to complete a comprehensive, multi-systemic assessment, treatment, and intervention plan with client-systems of all sizes and configurations.

1. Biological Dimension

AMS practitioners need to understand what some have called the "mind-body connection," or the links between social/emotional, behavioral, and potential biological or genetic issues that may be, at least in part, driving the problems presented by clients in practice. As scientific evidence mounts regarding the biological and genetic sources of personal troubles (i.e., some mental illness, etc.) it grows imperative for well-trained AMS practitioners to apply this knowledge in everyday work with clients (Ginsberg, Nackerud, & Larrison, 2004). The responsibility for understanding biology and physical health goes well beyond those working in direct health care practice settings (i.e., hospital, HIV, or hospice practice settings). Issues pertaining to physical health confront practitioners in all practice settings.

For example, practitioners working in mental health settings are confronted daily with issues pertaining to human biology; the sources and determinants of mental illness, differential uses of psychotropic medication, and often, the role played in client behavior by proper nutrition, appropriate health care, and even physical rest. In foster care and/or family preservation, practitioners also confront the effects of parental abuses (i.e., fetal alcohol syndrome [FAS]), medication management, and child/adolescent physical and biological development issues.

Beyond learning about the potential biological or physical determinants of various client troubles, having a keen understanding of the potential physical and health risks associated with various behaviors and/or lifestyles places practitioners in the position of intervening to save lives. For example, practitioners working with substance abusing or chemically dependent clients must understand drug pharmacology—especially drug-mixing—to predict potentially life-threatening physical withdrawal effects and/or to prevent intentional or unintentional harm caused by drug overdose (Johnson, 2004).

AMS requires that practitioners keep current with the latest information about human biology, development, genetics, and potential associated health risks facing clients and client-systems in practice. With that knowledge, practitioners can include this information during client assessment, treatment planning, and intervention strategies. It also requires practitioners to know the limits of professional responsibility. That is, social workers are not physicians and should never offer medical advice or guidance that is not supported by properly trained physicians. Therefore, AMS practitioners utilize the appropriate medical professionals as part of assessment, planning, and intervention processes with all clients.

2. Psychological/Emotional Dimension

AMS practitioners need a working knowledge of the ways that psychological and emotional functioning are intertwined with clients' problems and strengths, how issues from this dimension contribute to the way their client or client-system interacts with self and others in their environment, and how their environments influence their psychological and emotional functioning. There are several important skill sets that practitioners must develop to consider issues in this dimension. First, being able to recognize potential problems through a mental screening examination is a skill necessary to all practitioners. Also, having a keen understanding of the *Diagnostic and Statistical Manual of Mental Disorders* (DSM) (American Psychological Association, 2000), including the multi-axial diagnostic process, and recognition of the limits of this tool in the overall multi-systemic assessment process is instrumental. Especially critical is the ability to recognize co-occurring disorders (Johnson, 2004). It is also valuable to learn the Person-in-Environment (PIE) assessment system (Karls & Wandrei, 1994a, 1994b), a diagnostic model developed specifically for social workers to incorporate environmental influences.

In addition to understanding how psychology and emotion affects client mood and behavior, AMS practitioners also know how to employ different theories and models used for treating psychological and emotional functioning problems in the context of a client's multi-systemic assessment and treatment plan. This includes methods of treating individuals, families, and groups. Depending on the client's multi-systemic assessment, each of these modalities or some combination of modalities is appropriate for people with problems in this dimension.

3. Family Dimension

The family is the primary source of socialization, modeling, and nurturing of children. Hence, the family system has a significant impact on people's behavior, and people's behavior has significant impact on the health and well-being of their family system (Johnson, 2004). By integrating a family systems perspective into AMS, practitioners will often be able to make sense of behavior attitudes, beliefs, and values that would otherwise be difficult to understand or explain.

For our purposes, a family is defined as a group of people—regardless of their actual blood or legal relationship—whom clients consider to be members of their family (Johnson, 2004). This definition is designed to privilege clients' perceptions and subjective construction of reality and avoid disagreements over who is or is not in someone's family. So, if a client refers to a neighbor as "Uncle Joe," then that perception represents their reality. What good would it do to argue otherwise? Just as in client engagement discussed earlier, AMS practitioners seek to understand and embrace their client's unique definition of family, rather than imposing a rigid standard that may not fit their perceived reality. This is especially important when dealing with gay and lesbian clients. The law may not recognize gay or lesbian marriage, but AMS practitioners must, if that is the nature of the client's relationship and consistent with their belief system.

It is important to have a working knowledge of different theories and approaches to assessing and treating families and couples, as well as the ability to construct three-generation genograms to help conceptualize family systems and characterize the relationships that exist within the family system and between the family and its environment. Family treatment requires unique skills, specialized post-graduate training, and regular supervision before a practitioner can master the methods and call himself a "family therapist." However, the journey toward mastery is well worth it. Family treatment can be among the most effective and meaningful treatment modalities, often used in conjunction with other modalities (individual and/or group treatment), or as the primary treatment method.

4. Religious/Spiritual/Existential Dimension

Practitioners, students, and social work educators are often wary of exploring issues related to religion and spirituality in practice or the classroom. While there are exceptions, this important dimension often goes unexamined. Exploring people's religious beliefs and/or the tenets of their faith, even if they do not appear to have faith of spiritual beliefs, as they pertain to people's subjective definition of self in relation to the world, is an important part of AMS practice.

How clients view themselves in relation to others and their world provides an interesting window into the inner workings of their individual interpretation of culture. The extent that clients have internalized messages (positive, negative, and/or neutral) about their behavior from their faith community or personal spiritual belief systems can lead to an understanding of why people approach their lives and others in the ways they do. Moreover, much can be learned, based on these beliefs, about people's belief in the potential for change, how change occurs, and whom is best suited to help in that change process (if anyone at all), especially as it relates to the many moral and religious messages conveyed about people with problems.

Examination of this dimension goes beyond discovering which church or synagogue clients attend. It is designed to learn how and by what means clients define themselves and their lives in their worlds. What tenets they use to justify their lives, and how these tenets either support their current lives or can be used to help lead them toward change. There is much to be learned about client culture, how people interpret their culture in daily life, and how they view their life in their personal context from an examination of their religious or spiritual beliefs.

Moreover, religious and spiritual belief systems can also be a source of strength and support when considered in treatment plans. For example, while many clients may benefit from attendance at a community support group (i.e., Alcoholics Anonymous, Overeaters Anonymous, etc.) or professional treatment, some will benefit even more from participation in groups and events through local houses of worship. In our experience, many clients unable to succeed in professional treatment or support groups found success through a connection or reconnection with organizations that share their faith, whatever that faith may be.

5. Social/Environmental Dimension

Beyond the individual and family, AMS practitioners look to the client's community, including the physical environment, for important clues to help with engagement, assessment, and intervention planning. People live in communities comprised of three different types: (1) location (neighborhoods, cities, and rural or urban villages), (2) identification (religion, culture, race, etc.), and (3) affiliation (group memberships, subcultures, professional, political/ideological groups, etc.). There are five subdimensions that comprise the social/environmental dimension and incorporate the three types of communities listed above (Johnson, 2004):

1. Local community. This includes learning about physical environment, living conditions, a person's fit within her community, neighborhoods, where and how people live on a daily basis, and how they believe they are treated and/or accepted by community members and the community's power structure (i.e., the police, etc.).

2. Cultural context. This includes learning about clients' larger culture, their individual interpretation of culture, and how it drives or influences their daily life. Also included here is an exploration of histories of oppression and discrimination (individual, family, and community) and a client's subcultural group membership (i.e., drug culture, gang culture, etc.).

3. Social class. Often overlooked by practitioners, "information about people's social class is directly related to information about their families, the goodness-of-fit between the person and environment, and the strengths, resources, and/or barriers in their communities" (Johnson, 2004, p. 226). Some believe that no other demographic factor explains so extensively the differences between people and/or groups (Lipsitz, 1997; Davis & Proctor, 1989). Social class represents a combination of income, education, occupation, prestige, and community. It encompasses how these factors affect people's relative wealth and access to power and opportunity (Johnson, 2004).

4. Social/relational.   Human beings are social creatures who define themselves in relation to others (Johnson, 2004). Therefore, it is necessary to know something about people's ability to relate to others in their social environment. This investigation includes loved ones, friends, peers, supervisors, teachers, and others that they relate to in their daily life.

5. Legal history and involvement.   Obviously, this subdimension includes information about involvement with the legal system, by the client, family members, and friends and peers. More than recording a simple demographic history, seek to discover their feelings, attitudes, and beliefs about themselves, their place in the world, and how their brushes with the law fit into or influence their worldview.

6. Community resources.   Investigate the nature and availability of organizational support, including the role of social service organizations, politics, and your presence as a social worker in a client's life. For example, can clients find a program to serve their needs, or what does seeing a social worker mean within their community or culture? What are the conditions of the schools and the influence of churches, neighborhood associations, and block clubs? More importantly, what is the prevailing culture of the local environment? Are neighbors supportive or afraid of each other, and can a client expect to reside in the present situation and receive the support needed to change?

Be sure to include the professional helping system in this subdimension. Practitioners, their agencies, and the policies that assist or impede the professional helping process join with client-systems as part of the overall system in treatment. In other words, we must consider ourselves as part of the system—we do not stand outside in objective observation. This includes practitioner qualities and styles, agency policies, broader policies related to specific populations, and reimbursement policies, including managed care. All of these factors routinely influence the extent to which clients receive help, how clients are perceived in the helping system and, in the case of reimbursement policies, the method of treatment clients are eligible to receive regardless of how their multi-systemic assessment turns out.

Familiarity with various theories and models of community provide the keys to understanding the role of the social, physical, political, and economic environment in an individual's life. Community models look at the broader environment and its impact on people. Clients or client-systems with issues located in this dimension often respond well to group and family treatment methods. Occasionally, practitioners will be required to intervene at the local neighborhood or community level through organizing efforts and/or personal or political advocacy. For example:

> I (Johnson) was treating a client in individual and occasional family treatment when it was discovered that the daughter had been molested by a neighbor. The parents had not

reported the molestation. I soon learned that this neighbor was rumored to have molested several young girls in the neighborhood and that nobody was willing to report the molestations. I urged my client to organize a neighborhood meeting of all involved parents at her home. I served as the group facilitator for an intense meeting that ultimately built the community support needed to involve law enforcement. Within days, all of the parents in this group met with law enforcement. The perpetrator was arrested, convicted, and sentenced to life imprisonment.

6. Macro Dimension

AMS practitioners do not stop looking for relevant client information at the local level. They also look for clues in the way that macro issues influence clients, their problems, and potential for change. Knowledge of various laws (local, state, and national) are critical, as well as an understanding of how various social policies are interpreted and enforced in a particular client's life. For example, AMS requires an understanding of how child welfare policies affect the life of a chemically dependent mother, how healthcare policy affects a family's decisions about seeking medical treatment for their children, or how local standards of hygiene or cleanliness affect a family's status and acceptance in their community.

Issues to consider at this level also include public sentiment, stereotypes, and mechanisms of oppression that play a significant role in the lives of people who are not Caucasian, male, middle-class (or more affluent) citizens. Racism, classism, homophobia, and sexism, to name a few, are real threats to people who are attempting to live a "normal" life. An AMS practitioner must understand this reality and learn from clients what their individual perceptions are of these mechanisms and how they affect their problems and potential for change. The macro dimension involves issues such as housing, employment, and public support, along with the dynamics of the criminal justice system. For example, if clients have been arrested for domestic violence, what is the chance they will get fair and just legal representation? If they have been convicted and served jail or prison sentences, what are the chances they will have a reasonable chance of finding sufficient employment upon release?

These issues can be addressed in individual, family, or group treatments. Often, group treatment is an effective way to address issues clients struggle with at the macro level. Group treatment provides clients a way to address these issues in the context of mutual social support and a sense of belonging, helping them realize that they are not alone in their struggles (Yalom, 1995). AMS practitioners also recognize the need for political advocacy and community organizing methods for clients who present with consistent struggles with issues at the macro level.

Summary

The hallmark of AMS is its reliance on and integration of multi-systemic client information into one, comprehensive assessment, treatment, and intervention plan.

It incorporates knowledge, skills, and values from multiple sources, and relies on various sources of knowledge to paint a holistic picture of people's lives, struggles, strengths and resources, and potentials for change. Practitioners need a current working knowledge of human behavior, social systems theories, the latest social research and practice evaluation results, the impact of public laws and policies, as well as the skills and abilities to plan and implement treatment approaches as needed, in a manner consistent with our definition of informed eclecticism.

Many students new to AMS start out confused because the requirements seem so diverse and complicated. However, as you will see in the case presentations to follow, an organized and efficient practitioner who has learned to think and act multi-systemically can gather large amounts of critically important information about a client in a relatively short period. For this to happen, you must have a deep understanding of various theories, models, and practice approaches that address the various systemic levels considered and be willing to accept that no single model is completely right or wrong. It is always easier to latch on to one model and "go with it." However, the goal of practice is not to be correct or to promote your own ease and comfort, but to develop an assessment and treatment plan that is right for each client, whether or not you would ever use it in your own life. Social work practice is not about the social worker, but the client. It is important never to lose sight of this fact.

Bibliography

American Psychiatric Association. (2000). *Diagnostic and statistical manual of mental disorders* (4th ed.-TR). Washington, DC: Author.

Appleby, G. A. (2001). Dynamics of oppression and discrimination. In G. A. Appleby, E. Colon, & J. Hamilton (eds.), *Diversity, oppression, and social functioning: Person-in-environment assessment and intervention.* Boston: Allyn and Bacon.

Best, S., & Kellner, D. (1991). *Postmodern theory: Critical interrogations.* New York: Guilford Press.

Cournoyer, B. R. (2004). *The evidence-based social work skills book.* Boston: Allyn and Bacon.

Cox, E. O., & Parsons, R. J. (1994). *Empowerment-oriented social work practice with the elderly.* Pacific Grove, CA: Brooks/Cole.

Davis, L. E., & Proctor, E. K. (1989). *Race, gender, and class: Guidelines for practice with individuals, families, and groups.* Englewood Cliffs, NJ: Prentice-Hall.

Derezotes, D. S. (2000). *Advanced generalist social work practice.* Thousand Oaks, CA: Sage.

Fong, R. (2001). Culturally competent social work practice: Past and present. In R. Fong & S. Furuto (eds.), *Culturally competent practice: Skills, interventions, and evaluations.* Boston: Allyn and Bacon.

Freire, P. (1993). *Pedagogy of the oppressed.* New York: Continuum.

Gambrill, E. (1997). *Social work practice: A critical thinker's guide.* New York: Oxford University Press.

Gambrill, E. (1990). *Critical thinking in clinical practice.* San Francisco: Jossey-Bass.

Gaston, L. (1990). The concept of the alliance and its role in psychotherapy: Theoretical and empirical considerations. *Psychotherapy, 27,* 143–153.

Geertz, C. (1973). *The interpretation of cultures.* New York: Basic Books.

Germain, C. B., & Gitterman, A. (1996). *The life model of social work practice* (2nd ed.). New York: Columbia University Press.

Germain, C. B., & Gitterman, A. (1980). *The ecological model of social work practice.* New York: Columbia University Press.

Gibbs, L. E. (2003). *Evidence-based practice for the helping professions: A practical guide with integrated multimedia.* Pacific Grove, CA: Brooks/Cole.

Ginsberg, L., Nackerud, L., & Larrison, C. R. (2004). *Human biology for social workers: Development, ecology, genetics, and health.* Boston: Allyn and Bacon.

GlenMaye, L. (1998). Empowerment of women. In L. M. Gutierrez, R. J. Parsons, & E. O. Cox (eds.), *Empowerment in social work practice: A sourcebook.* Pacific Grove, CA: Brooks/Cole.

Gordon, J. U. (1993). A culturally specific approach to ethnic minority young adults. In E. M. Freeman (ed.), *Substance abuse treatment: A family systems perspective.* Newbury Park, CA: Sage.

Greif, G. L. (1986). The ecosystems perspective "meets the press." *Social Work, 31,* 225–226.

Harper, K. V., & Lantz, J. (1996). *Cross-cultural practice: Social work practice with diverse populations.* Chicago: Lyceum Books.

Johnson, J. L. (2004). *Fundamentals of substance abuse practice.* Pacific Grove, CA: Brooks/Cole.

Johnson, J. L. (2000). *Crossing borders—Confronting history: Intercultural adjustment in a post-Cold War world.* Lanham, MD: University Press of America.

Karls, J., & Wandrei, K. (1994a). *Person-in-environment system: The PIE classification system for functioning problems.* Washington, DC: NASW.

Karls, J., & Wandrei, K. (1994b). *PIE manual: Person-in-environment system: The PIE classification system for social functioning.* Washington, DC: NASW.

Kozol, J. (1991). *Savage inequalities: Children in America's schools.* New York: Crown Publishers.

Leigh, J. W. (1998). *Communicating for cultural competence.* Boston: Allyn and Bacon.

Lipsitz, G. (1997). Class and class consciousness: Teaching about social class in public universities. In A. Kumar (ed.), *Class issues.* New York: New York University Press.

Longres, J. F. (2000). *Human behavior in the social environment* (3rd ed.). Itasca, IL: F.E. Peacock.

Lum, D. (1999). *Culturally competent practice.* Pacific Grove, CA: Brooks/Cole.

McLaren, P. (1995). *Critical pedagogy and predatory culture: Oppositional politics in a postmodern era.* London: Routledge.

Miley, K. K., O'Melia, M., & DuBois, B. (2004). *Generalist social work practice: An empowerment approach.* Boston: Allyn and Bacon.

Miller, W. R., & Rollnick, S. (2002). *Motivational interviewing: Preparing people to change addictive behavior* (2nd ed.). New York: Guilford Press.

Mills, C. W. (1959). *The sociological imagination.* New York: Oxford University Press.

Parsons, R. J., Gutierrez, L. M., & Cox, E. O. (1998). A model for empowerment practice. In L. M. Gutierrez, R. J. Parsons, & E. O. Cox (eds.), *Empowerment in social work practice: A sourcebook.* Pacific Grove, CA: Brooks/Cole.

Pinderhughes, E. (1989). *Understanding race, ethnicity, and power.* New York: Free Press.

Popper, K. R. (1994). *The myth of the framework: In defense of science and rationality.* Edited by M. A. Notturno. New York: Routledge.

Saleebey, D. (2002). *The strengths perspective in social work practice* (3rd ed.). Boston: Allyn and Bacon.

Smelser, N. J. (1992). Culture: Coherent or incoherent. In R. Munch & N. J. Smelser (eds.), *Theory of culture.* Berkeley, CA: University of California Press.

Timberlake, E. M., Farber, M. Z., & Sabatino, C. A. (2002). *The general method of social work practice: McMahon's generalist perspective* (4th ed.). Boston: Allyn and Bacon.

van Wormer, K., & Davis, D. R. (2003). *Addiction treatment: A strengths perspective.* Pacific Grove, CA: Brooks/Cole.

Yalom, I. (1995). *The theory and practice of group psychotherapy* (4th ed.). New York: Basic Books.

2

Oliver

Catherine Simmons

This case study involves an early-middle-age male approaching military retirement. His initial symptoms were consistent with major depressive disorder, phase of life concerns, and partner relationship problems. I implemented a treatment approach using a four-session psycho-educational class followed by individual counseling, yet, as is often the case when a disconnection exists between treatment and clients, Oliver experienced no decrease in symptoms. During our fifth session, Oliver "came clean" by confiding that he had a significant alcohol dependency problem. From his revelation, we developed a more accurate therapeutic assessment and treatment plan. Although we tried a number of approaches to help Oliver overcome alcohol, a pattern of denial fueled by his desire to continue drinking thwarted the best efforts of a number of treatment agents. In the end, Oliver was simply not willing to take the steps necessary to stop drinking and change his life.

As is often true, Oliver's case was interesting because of its unexceptional nature. The issues clients bring to social workers in the beginning of the helping process are often merely the tip of the iceberg. By working with these issues at the beginning of the therapeutic relationship (starting where the client is), social workers establish trust with clients that help them deal with their deeper, often hidden, problems that frequently reveal themselves in later stages of the helping process (Shulman, 1999). In Oliver's case, his presenting concerns of depression and relationship problems hid his real problem—alcoholism.

Denial, dishonesty in the assessment and treatment process, change of diagnosis, hidden relapse events, issues pertaining to his family and employers, and determining what constituted a treatment failure were only a few of the social work issues we addressed in this case study. All of these issues are common for people working with clients who abuse or are dependent on substances (Mooney,

Eisenberg, & Eisenberg, 1992; Schuckit, 1995). Often clients present themselves to social work programs with very different concerns than their true underlying problem. At some point in the process, practitioners must become aware of these underlying issues and make critical decisions about how to proceed. By studying the assessment and treatment process we used with Oliver, readers can become aware of key issues so they can manage similar situations in their practice settings.

Questions

1. If you were the practitioner preparing to work with Oliver, what unique environmental or systemic issues would be involved given that the case takes place in a military environment?

2. How does this context affect the way that you would approach your client?

Client Information

Linking Theory to Practice

It is important for practitioners to link theory and practice during the helping process. Theory provides a map that guides practitioners through their day-to-day interactions with clients. Defined as "a group of related hypothetical concepts and constructs based on facts and observations that attempt to explain a particular phenomenon" (Barker, 1999, p. 100), theory provides support for the actions practitioners take in practice. "A strong theory provides a framework in which to understand some aspect of reality in a manner that permits the taking of actions for which one is prepared to be held accountable. A theory is not a body of dogma but a body of tested knowledge" (Turner, 1996, p. 2258). Theories form the foundation on which to build responsible professional practice.

It is important to remember that theories provide the foundation for practice, but do not come in one-size-fits-all packages. To treat client issues, practitioners can use a number of different theoretical orientations. For many practitioners, a cognitive behavioral approach is useful. Cognitive behavioral therapies (CBT) are "approaches to treatment using selected concepts and techniques from behaviorism, social learning theory, action therapy, functional school of social work, task centered treatment and therapies based on cognitive models" (Barker, 1999, p. 84). CBT is often time-limited, focusing on the present by setting goals that are specific to the client's presenting problem (Barker, 1999). For others, an insight-oriented treatment approach is more appropriate. Insight-oriented therapies are "treatment approaches oriented to helping individuals achieve greater self-awareness and understanding of their own conscious and unconscious motivations, emotions, thought processes, and underlying behaviors" (Barker, 1999, p. 242). Insight-oriented therapies are often long-term, focusing on the client's historical psychosocial development by setting broad general goals. We integrated several theories in our work with Oliver.

Oliver's presenting problems of depression, change of life issues, partner relationship problems, and relationship problems with others worked together to create his overall feeling of unhappiness. From his initial presentation, these problems appeared to be his primary issues and were addressed during the assessment and treatment processes. As is common with many clients, while addressing the presenting problems, other issues emerged. However, Oliver's presenting problems were simply the tip of the iceberg.

Intake Process

At the urging of his wife and supervisor, Oliver attended a 90-minute intake appointment with me at our multi-disciplinary outpatient mental health clinic. The clinic provides both short and long-term counseling to individuals and families with a variety of mental health and substance abuse concerns. Oliver was a 43-year-old Caucasian male working as a warehouse manager in a military organization. He was 5'11" with a slender to medium build and brown hair, slightly thinning, worn in a military haircut. He was clean-shaven and dressed neatly. Oliver was raised in a small midwestern town where he graduated from high school and worked as a warehouse stockperson until joining the military at the age of 20. His formal education included both military training and a few college classes. Ten years earlier, the Community College of the Air Force awarded him his associates' degree in business based on his military education, practical experience, and the college classes he completed. Spiritually, Oliver denied having a relationship with God, yet he attended a Catholic church with his wife weekly. His wife of 16 years was a Philippine national and they had no children.

At the time of his initial presentation to the clinic, Oliver had 23 years of military service and intended to retire in 12 months. Following retirement, he and his wife were planning to move to a small village in the Philippines, build a house, and live off his military pension. Geographically, this would enable them to live close to her family and provide Oliver and his wife the stability they had not experienced during his military career. Oliver denied having financial or medical related problems. He claimed that he had significant savings and would receive a comfortable pension with full medical benefits. Additionally, by living in the Philippines where the cost of living was significantly less, his retirement would amply provide for their financial needs. Overall, Oliver believed that his life was "falling into place." However, he did not understand many of the feelings he was experiencing.

Oliver denied any history of previous treatment, indicating that he made and attended this appointment only at the urging of his wife and immediate supervisor who "are worried" about his moodiness and problems getting along with others. Considering himself the "typical man" who "works hard" and takes care of his own problems, attending this appointment was a difficult step for him to take. Despite this difficulty, he talked frankly about many of his problems while engaging with me in an appropriate manner.

Strengths Perspective

The biopsychosocial assessment focused on the strengths perspective and included spirituality, family-of-origin, family-of-creation, medical concerns, mental health history, childhood and adult abuse history, substance use, current symptoms, duration of problems, coping skills, and social supports. The strengths perspective is "an orientation in social work and other professional practices that emphasizes the client's resources, capabilities, support systems and motivations to meet challenges and overcome adversity" (Barker, 1999, p. 468). In practice, this does not mean ignoring the existence of social problems and dysfunctions (Barker, 1999). Instead, it emphasizes client strengths in the process of achieving and maintaining their individual well-being. For Oliver, this meant us helping him to link his strengths to ways he could change his problems. Oliver's strengths included a supportive wife and work environment, financial security, personal organization, multiple personal achievements, a history of positive relationships with others (despite current problems), and a spoken desire to "fix" his problems.

One way that we used the strengths perspective with Oliver was to link his past successful interpersonal experiences to ways he had recently changed and to ways that he could improve his current relationships. Additionally, we elicited the support of his wife and supervisor, tying Oliver's future goals to his current activities, and allowing him take charge of his own feelings. The strengtha perspective is an important way to approach clients that begins during the intake assessment.

Substance Use

Oliver denied significant concerns in many areas of the biopsychosocial assessment. He denied having any medical problems and any history of physical, emotional, and/or sexual abuse. He also denied all substance-related misuse, stating that he "drinks only occasionally, at social events" and "never" touches illegal drugs. As confirmed by periodic drug testing, he had no history of illegal drug use. However, there was no system in place to ensure that his drinking history was accurate. Still, at that point in our professional relationship, I had no reason to doubt his statements.

The issue of substance use in the military is interesting. They handle illegal and prescription drug abuse quickly and decisively through random drug testing. When any illegal drug and/or not prescribed prescription drug use is identified, the person is generally taken through a military legal process called a court martial and then incarcerated and/or discharged from the military under the zero tolerance policy. On the other hand, the military treats alcohol use differently. Drinking is frequently encouraged at military social functions and many people in the military ignore minor alcohol-related infractions. However, when individuals develop alcohol problems that affect their job performance or otherwise embarrass their command, they are referred for substance abuse counseling. Although all five branches of uniformed service encourage help-seeking behavior, many people believe that they are stigmatized by enrolling in substance abuse programs. In cases of identified alcohol abuse and dependence where the client does not succeed in treatment, they must be discharged from the military. Many of these issues were not important to Oliver's intake assessment because he reported a neutral drinking history. However, they became very important later in the treatment process.

Presenting Problems and Initial Diagnoses

Oliver reported persistent symptoms of chronic fatigue, depressed mood, loss of interest in social activities, hypersomnia, and diminished concentration. He reported that his symptoms had lasted for more than six months. He also reported having frequent arguments with his wife and coworkers. In Oliver's words, he "wasn't getting along with anyone anymore." Additionally, he believed that his symptoms were becoming progressively worse.

The symptoms Oliver described were congruent with the diagnosis of Major Depressive Disorder, Single Episode (APA, 2000). A Major Depressive Episode is indicated when clients meet the following DSM-IV-TR criteria: (a) a depressed mood most of the day, nearly every day, (b) markedly diminished interest in all activities, (c) insomnia, (d) fatigue, (e) feelings of worthlessness, and (f) diminished ability to concentrate (APA, 2000). His symptoms did not stem from bereavement and affected Oliver's ability to function both personally and professionally. During the assessment and the initial stage of treatment, Oliver denied substance abuse issues and indicated that this was the first time he had ever experienced depressive symptoms.

Oliver's symptoms concerned him. He was not sure how to handle these feelings because he had "never experienced anything like this before." The distress Oliver had about his out-of-control thoughts and moods exacerbated his depressive symptoms, causing him to withdraw from many aspects of his life. Although he denied current and past suicidal thoughts, feelings, and plans by stating, "I will never kill myself," he also believed that his problems were never going away. From his initial presentation and based on the client data described above, I believed it was appropriate to accept the diagnosis of Major Depressive Disorder, Single Episode and proceed to the treatment planning stage. However, to provide quality treatment, Oliver's pending retirement and his interpersonal and partner relationship problems needed exploration.

Pending Retirement

Oliver discussed his impending retirement with mixed emotions. For the past six months, he reported difficulty "getting along" with his colleagues. This made him look forward to "leaving that place." Additionally, he spent 23 years moving around the world in the military and was excited about settling in one location. Oliver and his wife owned property in his wife's village where there existed a large U.S. expatriate community. For the past 10 years, he and his wife had been planning to build a "dream house" where Oliver would continue to have exposure to U.S. culture while improving his standard of living and giving his wife a chance to return to her native culture. Additionally, Oliver reported having a good relationship with his in-laws and was excited about getting to know his wife's family better. Overall, the positives related to his upcoming retirement were strengths in Oliver's life.

Despite these strengths, Oliver also reported experiencing some mild anxiety about his future. Inherent with marrying outside of one's nationality are concerns about one member living outside of their familiar culture (Devore & Schlesinger, 1999). For the first 16 years of their marriage, his wife lived with him in the United States. Oliver believed that it was "only fair" to move to the Philippines because he had taken his wife away from her family for so long. He stated that moving there after retirement was "the right thing to do." However, he also reported a desire to "move back to the midwest someday." Apparent in his life choices were two opposing desires. On one hand, he wanted to move to his wife's village, and on the other, he wanted to return to his childhood community. I believe this dilemma contributed to his presenting problems.

Additionally, Oliver expressed remorse about leaving the military. He liked the thought of not having to work anymore, but also liked the structure and pride that came with his job. He believed that there was a sense of belonging and being important in the service that he would lose when he retired. The sense of impending loss combined with mixed emotions is common among individuals approaching retirement (Shulman, 1999). While discussing these life changes, Oliver expressed many feelings including fear, sorrow, regret, worry, excitement, and joy. These "phase of life" contradictions were important diagnostic and treatment issues for consideration. For this reason, adding a diagnosis of Phase of Life problem was appropriate (APA, 2000).

The DSM-IV-TR (APA, 2000) classifies Phase of Life problems as a V-code, listed under conditions that may be a focus of clinical attention. This category of diagnoses covers conditions that are important to address in treatment because they are common reasons that people seek services but are not specific mental illness (Barker, 1999). V-code diagnoses can be used when (a) a client has no mental health diagnosis but has distress in the area indicated by the V-code, (b) has a mental health diagnosis that is not related to the area indicated by the V-code, or (c) has a mental health diagnosis that is related to the area indicated by the V-code but the problem is significantly severe to warrant independent clinical attention (APA, 2000). Phase of Life problems "can be used when the focus of clinical attention is a problem associated with a particular developmental phase" (APA, 2000, p. 742). Although Oliver's primary diagnosis, Major Depressive Disorder, Single Episode is a mental disorder, his Phase of Life problem was significant enough to warrant clinical attention.

Relationship Problems

Oliver reported a two-year history of frequent arguments and disconnections with his family members and friends. He believed that he "has no friends left." Throughout the years, he had a number of close friendships. However, in the two years leading up to our session he had lost contact with most of them. Additionally, Oliver had not spoken to anyone in his family-of-origin for three years. He believed that it was easier to have no friends because they could not drift out of his life after minor disagreements. Because of these interpersonal problems, Oliver spent much of his time alone. Through discussing his recent history of interpersonal problems, Oliver concluded that his problem getting along with others was both a symptom and cause of his depression.

His interpersonal problems seemed progressive. Until five years earlier, Oliver had no trouble getting along with people. He and his wife rarely fought and he got along well with his peers and supervisors. Through attending church activities and participating in hobbies such as golf and martial arts, he had a number of friends. In the course of the intake discussion, Oliver could not remember when his difficulties began, but notes that over the previous two years, his problems had grown progressively worse. He also stated that he wanted to work on these problems in therapy.

Marital Problems

In addition to his problems with friendship, Oliver's relationship with his wife was the worst it had ever been. Their arguments were frequent and mostly related to "things I have not done." He believed that she "nags" him all the time, which caused him to "tune out" what she was saying. Although he believed that many of her concerns were warranted, he did not know how to change or fix them. For Oliver, "turning off" his emotions and "checking out" was a coping skill that protected him from feelings he was unable to deal with. His reliance on this coping mechanism was negatively affecting his marriage.

Despite their communication problems, Oliver denied any potential for divorce, stating that neither he nor his wife would ever "ask for it." Divorce was not acceptable to his wife because of her religious beliefs and family. In her family-of-origin, getting a divorce was considered a disgrace that would cause her to "lose face." Her Roman Catholic religious affiliation also discouraged divorce. Since she was highly enmeshed in these two systems, asking for a divorce was not a viable option. This tied her to Oliver "for better and worse." Oliver stated that divorce was not a viable option for him because he "has already made that mistake once." This was Oliver's second marriage. When asked to discuss his first marriage and divorce in more detail, he said that they were both "too young" when they were married, further suggesting that there were communication concerns and infidelity by both parties. Oliver did not want to re-experience his past hurts. He stated that one of his goals for therapy was to make his marriage strong again. Oliver's issues in his marriage warranted the V-code Partner Relationship Problem (APA, 2000).

Family-of-Origin

Oliver is the youngest child in a family of four. He said he was a "bonus baby" because he was 17 years younger than his next closest sibling was. His parents were over 50 years old when they had him. He portrayed a distant relationship between himself and his siblings, stating that there was "nothing wrong" with his siblings, he simply did not relate well with them. While growing up, his parents had problems keeping up with him, often opting out of contributing to events that he participated in (e.g., Little League and the Boy Scouts.) He did not think that his parents had substance-related problems, but did say that his dad had a drink every day. As a child, Oliver played sports, had a number of good friends, and received average grades in school. Although both of his parents passed away when he was thirty, Oliver felt that he used effective coping skills to work through their death.

From this point in the assessment process, I wanted to understand how Oliver's disconnection from his family-of-origin affected his life. He denied having one "big falling out event" that caused him to lose touch with his family. Instead, he related a number of small disagreements about things he "can't remember." Minimizing these events, Oliver described a lifelong pattern of disconnected relationships in his family. Going long periods without talking was their norm. I then addressed the extent to which his interactions with his family-of-origin were congruent with his withdrawal from his wife and others. Linking Oliver's interpersonal relationship problems to his family-of-origin helped him gain insight into his lifelong behavior patterns. Through this discussion, Oliver began to see that his coping mechanism of "checking out" had been a lifelong pattern that he learned while growing up.

Education as Part of the Intake Process

Providing educational materials during the intake process reinforces concepts introduced in the intake session and provides alternative explanations for the topics that most affect clients. By giving Oliver materials on depression, change of life issues, and communication, he was better able to engage in a more detailed discussion about many of the past strategies he used to overcome his problems (e.g., using stress management techniques, relaxation, and talking about his problems). The discussion led to ideas about how specific aspects of these strategies were not working for his current problems. (E.g., Oliver had stopped talking to his wife about his problems and feelings, causing additional stress on his marriage.) From understanding what had worked before and what was not working now, we generated ideas for intervention. This process is part of the strengths perspective discussed earlier. Focusing on Oliver's strengths helped him to verbalize the changes he needed to make in his life without feeling hopeless about himself and his problems.

Questions

The author has presented client data, along with her assessment and diagnoses based on that data. The author has also hinted that this information did not comprise Oliver's whole story. Given this information,

1. **Do you concur with the author's diagnoses? If not, what factors did you use to base your differing clinical opinion?**

2. **Make a list of Oliver's problems and strengths, including those you might identify that the author omitted.**

3. **Construct a three-generation genogram of Oliver's family system. What did this graphical representation of his family demonstrate to you that are helpful during assessment?**

4. **At this time, write a short narrative description that gives a holistic picture of Oliver as it pertains to your assessment and possible future treatment implications. Be sure to consider the military context and issues pertaining to client engagement.**

Preliminary Treatment Options

Oliver's symptoms appeared relatively mild and there were no clinical indications that he was holding back or denying underlying problems. His story appeared both honest and congruent. For this reason, we recommended individual, brief solution-focused therapy to help Oliver work on his issues of depression, interpersonal problems, and retirement. However, because Oliver found it difficult to accept help from others, he decided that he did not want or need individual counseling. He also refused to make an appointment with a psychiatrist for potential medication for his depression. Oliver believed that his problems were fixable without medication or individual therapy. Still, he did want to learn more about various coping skills that could help "bring him out of his funk."

In deciding the best course of treatment to meet Oliver's needs, we considered all of the clinic and community's resources. The mental health clinic offered a four-session psycho-educational class with a required one-session follow-up after completion of the class. For Oliver, this was a comfortable option. He could take the class, participate to the extent that he felt comfortable, and then follow-up with me in a month to consider other options. His primary goals were (a) to understand depression, (b) learn new coping skills, and (c) improve his communication with others. The class would help Oliver address these goals while working in his comfort zone.

Diagnosis and Treatment Plan

Our mental health clinic uses a managed care model. Within this system, similar to many managed care models across the United States, clients must meet several criteria before receiving services. Among the criteria are (1) preauthorization for services, (2) appropriate diagnosis for presenting symptoms, (3) having a treatment plan with congruent goals, and (4) progression toward those goals as determined through utilization review (Edinburg & Cottler, 1996). Because Oliver met the DSM-IV-TR criteria for Major Depressive Disorder, Single Episode in addition to the V-codes Partner Relationship Problems, Relationship Problems NOS, and Phase of Life Problems (APA, 2000), he was eligible for services in the mental health system. To ensure that clients understand their diagnosis, it is best to discuss with them both what the diagnoses are and why they meet the criteria before writing their treatment plan. In Oliver's case, I included this discussion in the educational portion of the intake assessment, waiting to address his treatment goals after he understood his diagnoses.

Because Oliver's treatment plan included only psycho-educational classes with one follow-up session, it was appropriate to discuss and write his treatment plan at the conclusion of the intake assessment. When we use higher levels of service, we usually write the treatment plan in session two or three, after clients have time to think about their goals. We include the type, frequency, and duration of treatment, and who will be involved in each aspect of treatment in the client's treatment plans (Granvold, 1994). Additionally, providing clients with a copy of their treatment plan helps to ensure that they understand the expectations and helps them feel that they are partners in the process. Following these steps in treatment planning gave Oliver a greater sense of control over his problems and his treatment.

Psycho-Educational Class

The psycho-educational class Oliver attended focused on cognitive behavioral coping strategies including the identification of thought distortions, methods of disrupting these distortions, and ways to change distorted thinking patterns. Theoretically, this class was based on the cognitive behavioral approach, emphasizing how thoughts lead to feelings and actions. By identifying and changing problematic thinking patterns, individuals can change the subsequent maladaptive feelings and behaviors. Learning how to replace their distorted thinking with new thoughts that contribute to more desirable actions are taught and practiced (Beck, 1967; Beck, 1988; Beck, Rush, Shaw & Emery, 1979; Burns, 1999; Greenberger & Padesky, 1995).

Oliver felt comfortable in the class, participated appropriately, and completed all of the homework assignments. From his participation in the group, he began to learn about himself and develop a greater sense of control over his mood. During the individual follow-up session, he indicated a desire to work further on his problems, claiming that he was "ready for individual counseling." At this follow-up session, Oliver continued to deny any other problems including past trauma and substance misuse. To help him organize his thoughts, I assigned a worksheet that focused on what he wanted to achieve in counseling. We ended the follow-up session with a temporary plan to meet again in one week to discuss his new treatment goals.

Questioning the Diagnosis and Treatment: Updating the Treatment Plan

Oliver had completed the worksheet by the time of our next session. He indicated that he wanted to work on the same goals that he addressed in the psycho-educational class: (1) understanding depression, (2) learning new coping skills, and (3) improving communication. Through discussion about his goals, Oliver revealed that he had additional concerns that he was "not ready to discuss yet." Although indicating that he understood the importance of readiness and openness to successful treatment outcome, Oliver stated that he simply "does not feel comfortable" talking about his underlying issues.

Clients often present with problems that they are not ready to address when they begin therapy (Shulman, 1999). Practitioners must "start where the client is" by respecting client wishes as they relate their hidden problems (Shulman, 1999). Knowing that patience and time are important components of the treatment process gives clients the opportunity to reveal their hidden problems when they are ready (Shulman, 1999). Respecting Oliver's desires, we updated his treatment plan to include individual counseling to work toward achieving his three goals.

Follow-Up Sessions

From this updated treatment plan, I conducted two additional sessions that focused on the issues Oliver agreed to work on. We held the fourth session conjointly with Oliver's wife to address communication issues using the PREP model, a speaker-listener technique. This technique requires listeners to repeat what the speakers stated before moving on to their own response. The listener then becomes the speaker, and the listener (who was the original speaker) repeats what they said and so on (Markman, Stanley, & Blumeburg, 1994). Despite the effectiveness both parties believed this exercise provided, neither addressed the proverbial "elephant in the living room." This unspoken problem was apparent through verbal and nonverbal tension felt during the session and Oliver's continued discomfort to reveal the "additional concerns" he alluded to in previous sessions.

Some practitioners would confront these underlying issues. However, I respected Oliver's lack of readiness and/or unwillingness because he was participating in treatment and appeared to be moving toward discussing his "additional concerns" on his own. I determined that confronting him at that point in the therapeutic relationship would be counterproductive. With Oliver's defense mechanism of "closing down," forcing him to reveal his hidden problems would have likely generated resistance and/or caused him to discontinue therapy altogether. It was important to start where he was and proceed from there, remembering that patience in practice often pays off by making clients feel safe, cared for, and willing to reveal their innermost secrets. At this point in the therapeutic relationship, Oliver was not ready to move past his original areas of concern. I respected his feelings.

It is important to note that each session included questions about the presence of suicidal and homicidal thoughts, domestic violence, the intensity of his symptoms, coping strategies, and substance use. Oliver denied safety concerns and substance use at each session. He also reported success with new coping skills in his life outside of therapy. Additionally, in the couple's session, his wife denied concerns related to domestic violence and Oliver's substance use, instead endorsing his positive use of more effective coping strategies since the beginning of treatment. From the incongruence between stated actions and continuing symptoms, it was apparent that there was something important underlying Oliver's behavior that was going unaddressed.

There are a number of reasons that client needs are not addressed in therapy. Three of the most common are (1) incongruence between therapeutic approach and client needs, (2) therapist and client incompatibility, and/or (3) client denial and/or distraction. Incongruence between therapeutic approach and client needs means that the therapeutic approach may not be appropriate for a particular client. Not all approaches work with all clients or meet all client needs (Payne, 1997). For example, the cognitive behavioral approach may not be appropriate for clients who want to analyze deeply held childhood issues (Granvold, 1994).

Therapist and client incompatibility means there is disconnection between the therapist and the client. Perhaps the client does not like a practitioner demographic category such as gender or ethnicity. Additionally, clients may feel uncomfortable with some aspect of the practitioner's style (Devore & Schlesinger, 1999).

Client denial and/or distraction occur when clients do not focus on the therapeutic change process for some reason. Denial is a "defense mechanism that protects the personality from anxiety or guilt by disavowing or ignoring unacceptable thoughts, emotions, or wishes" (Barker, 1999, p. 122). Distraction occurs when clients focus on aspects of their lives that are ignored in the therapeutic relationship. For example, if a client is having housing issues, he may be unable to focus on his depression. In Oliver's case, denial and distraction were the most likely candidates for why he was not progressing.

Changing the Diagnosis

At the beginning of the fifth session, Oliver "came clean" by reporting a significantly higher level of alcohol use than he originally described. Oliver conveyed that he had been dishonest about his drinking behavior and told his wife "not to talk about it" in their conjoint session. Following the session, the couple argued about his "dishonesty" in therapy. Oliver said that this argument led him to "be honest" now. He further revealed that he had been drinking 18 to 24 bottles of beer per night, every night for more than one year. He stated that he had tried to "cut down" or quit many times, but failed each time. He also stated that his depression, fatigue, marital, and interpersonal problems were related to his alcohol use. However, he also reported being "afraid" to address this in previous sessions. After completing an "honest" substance assessment, I found him to meet the criteria for both Alcohol Abuse and Dependence (APA, 2000).

Alcohol Abuse Symptoms

Our latest assessment indicated that Oliver met three of the four DSM-IV-TR criteria for substance abuse (APA, 2000). Oliver reported getting into significant trouble at work on numerous occasions over the course of the last year. This trouble included arriving late and doing incomplete work because he was hungover or intoxicated. He had frequent arguments with colleagues related to his job performance. His supervisor had assigned him a job he felt was demeaning to "keep him out of trouble" and had encouraged him to seek help on his own before being forced to seek help as a condition of employment. He admitted to driving and operating warehouse machinery after drinking, although he reported that he "never drinks and drives."

Additionally, he had frequent arguments with his wife about his drinking that became more intense when he was drunk. Since he was drunk most of the time, his marriage was strained. Despite knowing his problems related to drinking, Oliver continued drinking at increasing levels. He felt powerless over alcohol and wanted the problems related to his drinking to end. However, he also wanted to continue drinking. The desire to continue drinking despite problems in people's lives is common (Mooney, Eisenberg, & Eisenberg, 1992). It becomes like a dance the client does with himself or herself. They want to quit drinking, yet they also want to continue drinking. The symptoms Oliver described met the criteria for substance abuse.

Alcohol Dependence Symptoms

Oliver also met six of the seven DSM-IV-TR criteria for substance dependence (APA, 2000). His symptoms included (a) increased tolerance marked by a need for increased amounts to achieve the same effect and diminished effect with continued use, (b) use of larger than intended amounts over longer times than intended, and (c) a persistent desire yet inability to cut down and/or quit. Additionally, Oliver had ceased all social and recreational activities because of his drinking and dedicated most of his time to drinking or recovering from drinking.

Oliver could not remember one night in the six months prior to the assessment where he drank less than twelve bottles of beer. His typical evening entailed drinking three bottles before dinner. Because his appetite was usually small, he drank another four or five bottles at dinner. He then would drink six to twelve more bottles of beer while he watched television before falling asleep on his recliner. On many evenings, he tried to drink only one or two beers. However, his cravings always got the best of him, leading him to drink as much or more than usual. On days that he did not arrive home from work until later in the evening, he experienced tremors, anxiety, and nausea. Drinking beer was the only effective means he knew to relieve his withdrawal symptoms. He denied drinking "hard" liquor, claiming that his hangovers were worse after drinking liquor. However, he switched from light to regular beer five months earlier and, when that did not work, began drinking imported beer for the higher alcohol content. As stated above, he clearly met the DSM-IV-TR criteria for Alcohol Dependence (APA, 2000). When clients meet the criteria for abuse and dependence, they receive the more serious diagnosis (APA, 2000).

Medical Concerns with Alcohol Dependence

Immediately following the discovery of Oliver's alcoholism, he received a complete medical screening because he was at-risk for withdrawal syndrome. Oliver's physical assessment and toxicology screening indicated significant medical concerns including alcoholic hepatitis. Alcoholic hepatitis usually develops after many years of excessive drinking and is related to malnutrition caused by the empty calories in alcohol, reduced appetite, and malabsorption caused by the presence of alcohol in the liver. When these conditions exist, alcohol's toxicity produces liver inflammation, or hepatitis. Unchecked, hepatitis can progress to the more serious condition known as fatty liver and, finally, cirrhosis. Complications associated with this condition include alcoholic encephalopathy, damage to brain tissue, portal hypertension, and high blood pressure (Mooney, Eisenberg, & Eisenberg, 1992). Oliver's health was in jeopardy if he continued drinking.

Oliver's alcohol dependence played a significant role in all aspects of his life. Socially, Oliver was isolated. He had no friends to lean on and a considerably strained marriage. Professionally, he experienced a significant decrease in job performance leading his supervisors to worry about his "safety" at work. Medically, Oliver was at significant risk of dying. The professional and social concerns related to Oliver's drinking marked only the beginning of his journey. He had a long road ahead if he was serious about achieving sobriety.

Questions

As the author previously stated, this type of client presentation is common in substance abuse treatment. Often, clients will present with serious issues and the motivation to address them to distract practitioners away from their chemical dependency. The author decided to work with Oliver's presenting problems, while remaining vigilant about inconsistencies and incongruence in his stories. Ultimately, this led to Oliver revealing his alcohol dependence later in treatment. Some call this a harm reduction approach to treatment (Johnson, 2004). Assume for a moment that you were the practitioner, and you suspected that Oliver was hiding something.

1. What would your approach have been toward Oliver's refusal to divulge his alcohol dependence? Would you have chosen to take the approach of the author, or to take a different, perhaps more confrontational approach? Please

defend your decision with information from the practice literature, practice experience, and through discussions with student-colleagues.

2. Explore the practice literature for definitions of harm reduction, as it pertains to substance abuse and other treatment issues. Based on your reading and experience, state your position on harm reduction and provide a defense of your position.

Treatment Options for Alcohol Abuse/Dependence

Now that we had an accurate assessment and diagnosis of Oliver's problems, we could explore treatment options. The three levels of care are available to people with substance abuse problems: inpatient treatment, outpatient treatment, and day treatment (intensive outpatient). Inpatient treatment usually requires a 14- to 30-day stay in a hospital or other residential treatment facility. The modality of inpatient treatment is often education, individual therapy, and group therapy. With inpatient care, the client is isolated from the life she knew and given the opportunity to focus solely on recovery.

Outpatient treatment generally occurs in clinics, hospitals, or alcohol rehabilitation facilities. The client normally resides at home and participates in the program on a part-time basis during the day. The focus of outpatient treatment is generally on education using a group format and is most suitable for individuals with less severe substance problems.

An additional treatment option is day treatment, or intensive outpatient treatment. In this level of care, clients check into a facility all day but return home each night. The focus of day treatment is often education, in addition to individual and group therapy. It is usually similar in intensity and modality to inpatient treatment, except clients live and sleep at home instead of a hospital. Day treatment is less costly than inpatient programs because it does not require a hospital stay, but these programs are not always available and require clients to live in close proximity to the treatment program (Johnson, 2004).

Our mental health clinic had a comprehensive outpatient substance abuse program. However, because of Oliver's serious chemical dependency, outpatient care was not enough. We recommended an inpatient or day treatment program instead. Unfortunately, the local area did not have either "level of care" available nearby. The daily quantity of alcohol that Oliver consumed, coupled with the unavailability of a day treatment program, made traveling outside the local area for inpatient treatment the most viable choice. Following a discussion about treatment options, Oliver decided to think about what he was willing to do. Agreeing to go to an inpatient program required him to leave his comfort zone and make a commitment to work hard and get sober. This is often a tough decision for clients to make (Mooney, Eisenberg, & Eisenberg, 1992). Oliver did not want to go this route until he met with his medical provider and learned about the medical concerns caused by his drinking. After that meeting, he decided to attend inpatient treatment.

In Oliver's medical care system, finding an open treatment bed usually takes planning. Hence, I started the process before holding a treatment team meeting. Once we obtained a bed date, we could always cancel if the treatment team or client decided to go another route. However, if we waited to find a bed until after the team met, one may not be available. I contacted three inpatient treatment programs before finding an opening. Yet, the earliest opening I could find was in two weeks and the program required spousal participation during the final days of treatment, detoxification prior to admission, and was located a considerable distance away from Oliver's home. Despite these issues, Oliver agreed to the program's terms. Only then did I schedule a treatment team meeting to discuss this option with everyone involved in Oliver's case.

Bring the Systems Together to Plan Treatment

Treatment team meetings ensure that everyone involved in the client's life agree about the course of treatment. Oliver's treatment team included Oliver, his wife, his work supervisor, his physician, the substance abuse program staff, and me. Everyone on the team (including Oliver) agreed that Oliver's marriage, his retirement benefits, and his physical health were in jeopardy if he continued drinking. To be successful, Oliver needed the time and support to make his treatment program work. Hence, his supervisor gave him the time away from work and his wife agreed to participate in the spouse's portion of the inpatient program. The outpatient substance abuse clinic provided individual supportive services for the two weeks before Oliver's admission and arranged the initial, 72-hour "observation," or detoxification period prior to admission into inpatient treatment.

Detoxification Concerns

Oliver's condition required a hospital admission for detoxification to ensure that he did not experience significant withdrawal from alcohol, or die in the process. Since there was no way to ensure his sobriety for the two weeks, detoxification was especially important. Sudden withdrawal from alcohol can put the client's health at risk. Withdrawal usually begins 12 hours after the last drink and peaks at 48 to 72 hours. Symptoms of withdrawal include nervousness, shakiness, anxiety, irritability, emotional volatility, depression, fatigue, heart palpitations, headache, sweating, nausea, vomiting, insomnia, rapid heart rate, pupil dilation, clammy skin, hand and body tremors, and involuntary eyelid movements. At its worst, withdrawal can result in hallucinations, agitation, fever, convulsions, stroke, and even death (Mooney, Eisenberg, & Eisenberg, 1992). Because of the health risks, clients must withdraw under medical supervision. We arranged with his physician and HMO provider to have him admitted to the hospital for the immediate 72 hours prior to entering the inpatient program.

Inpatient Program

The inpatient program was located a significant distance from his home. This thirty-day program focused on confronting client denial systems and promoting lifestyle change through individual therapy, group therapy, self-help groups, psycho-educational classes, and communal living. It was located on the grounds of a hospital but separate from the traditional patient population. A typical day includes a 7 a.m. wake-up call followed by physical training and breakfast. Food preparation and cleanup are performed by the hospital staff. However, clients must make their own beds and clean the living area. Following breakfast, clients attend group therapy followed by a psycho-educational class and lunch. After lunch, they have individual therapy or free time with another psycho-educational class in the mid-afternoon. In addition to the structured activities, clients attend Alcoholics Anonymous (AA) daily and participate in the community. This model provides clients the opportunity to learn how to live a substance-free life without the distractions of their "everyday life." The last weekend of treatment includes family participation activities designed to transition the client back to the family and the family back to its "changed" loved one. Because of the change from active drinking to abstinence, family transition is a needed and important step in the treatment process.

In follow-up contacts with the clinic, Oliver's inpatient counselor reported that Oliver exhibited denial early in his stay. Since this is common in substance abuse treatment, it did not concern the counselor at first. After a number of confrontations in the first week, Oliver began participating in the program and the community. He met the criteria for graduation, finished the family weekend activities with his wife, and graduated on time. However, Oliver's counselor noted concerns about his potential for "gaming the system." In many substance abuse programs, clients take the superficial steps necessary to get through the program while not making the changes needed to succeed on their own. Clients do this so frequently that practitioners refer to it as "gaming the system." Oliver may have participated in all of the activities but the counselor was concerned that his "heart was not in it."

He graduated because he did everything required yet true lifestyle change may not have occurred. Because it took Oliver so long to "come clean" about his drinking in the first place, I was not surprised. True change is difficult and people with substance-related problems are often resistant to this because of the layers of denial they have created to protect their addiction (Mooney, Eisenberg, & Eisenberg, 1992). Regardless of where he was internally, Oliver graduated from the program and returned home to participate in an aftercare program designed to help him solidify the changes he made and help him progress in his recovery.

Aftercare Program

Oliver returned to aftercare at the substance abuse program of the mental health clinic. Aftercare helps to ease clients back into the "real world" after treatment. This phase of treatment can last up to one year and usually consists of individual thera-py, group counseling, education, and support groups such as AA or Rational Recovery. AA and Rational Recovery are voluntary self-help organizations of peo-ple who have experienced problems related to alcohol abuse and dependence (Mooney, Eisenberg, & Eisenberg, 1992). Both organizations focus on the need for total abstinence yet go about it in different ways. AA uses a twelve-step recovery process that includes admitting powerlessness over alcohol and relying on a higher spiritual power to assist with recovery (Mooney, Eisenberg, & Eisenberg, 1992). Rational Recovery does not use steps, believe in one's powerlessness, or focus on a higher spiritual power (Mooney, Eisenberg, & Eisenberg, 1992). Instead, Rational Recovery asks members to make a commitment to never drink or use drugs again by accepting themselves and focusing on their own inner strengths (Mooney, Eisenberg, & Eisenberg, 1992). Oliver's aftercare program included all of these components as well as spousal support and employer education.

During aftercare, Oliver struggled with his sobriety. He said that he "did not like" the inpatient program because he "didn't learn anything there." He also con-tinued to believe that he could manage his drinking (e.g., continue drinking in lim-ited quantities), that he did not need to achieve total abstinence. This is a common sign that a person has not accepted their problem with alcohol and "proof" that they have been "gaming the system." One of the first steps in substance abuse treatment is for clients to admit and accept that alcohol and other drugs are a problem in their life, one that they cannot control. By wanting to negotiate the terms of his sobriety, Oliver demonstrated that he was in denial. Denial is a defense mechanism many clients use to protect themselves from the short-term pain of admitting they have a problem (Mooney, Eisenberg, & Eisenberg, 1992). Only by eliminating denial and reaching a level of acceptance about the nature of one's problems can clients begin to expect to achieve sobriety. I believe it is the most important hurdle to cross in treatment.

AA introduced the idea of "steps" in the recovery process. In 1935, a recov-ering alcoholic named Bill Wilson, often referred to as Bill W, founded AA as a fel-lowship for people who wished to stop drinking. AA uses a twelve-step process to recovery and twelve traditions that provide the cornerstone for all AA groups around the world. People progress through the steps as they change their lives. The twelve-step model is successfully used with a number of addiction-related problems includ-ing Narcotics Anonymous (NA), Cocaine Anonymous (CA), Smokers Anonymous (SA), and Overeaters Anonymous (OA). Many treatment programs use this model or parts of this model in chemical dependency treatment (Mooney, Eisenberg, & Eisenberg, 1992).

Regardless of the treatment program or approach, recovery proceeds through three conceptual stages. The first is the stabilization stage. During this stage, clients become abstinent, accept their problem with substances, and commit to making changes (Smyth, 1996). In Oliver's case, he remained in this stage throughout his time in treatment. Regardless of the steps he took and the superficial changes he made, Oliver could not admit to himself that he had a problem with alcohol and needed to quit drinking. Throughout treatment, he maintained the idea that he could learn to control his drinking. Therefore, he never stopped drinking.

Questions

The author's position is that the only way to recover from chemical dependency is through abstinence. That is, clients must stop all substance use because it is not possible for chemically dependent people to return to controlled use. The author did not call dependence a disease, but attributed disease-like qualities to chemical dependency and used the major tenets of the disease model by requiring abstinence. Her position is consistent with the majority of the substance abuse field. However, the field is not unanimous. Several prominent authors and a growing body of research claims otherwise; that it is possible to achieve controlled use status.

1. Review the theory and practice literature to locate and analyze evidence on both sides of this issue. Following your review, what does the preponderance of the evidence say about the abstinence versus controlled drinking controversy?

2. How do the conclusions you derived from the literature compare to your personal and professional beliefs about the subject? What do your student-colleagues and/or instructors say about this issue?

3. How will you approach clients who come into your care demanding that you help them learn to drink or use drugs in a controlled way?

The second stage of recovery is the rehabilitation stage. This stage focuses on helping clients establish drug-free lifestyles and identities. The third stage, maintenance, focuses on solidifying gains made in treatment, preventing relapse, and preparing clients for termination (Smyth, 1996). While Oliver participated in second-stage activities, his behavior and attitude suggested that he never moved past the first stage in the recovery process.

Hence, Oliver had multiple relapses during the first three weeks of aftercare. Following his second admitted relapse, the treatment team reconvened to discuss Oliver's progress. His relapses were negatively affecting his home life, work life, and had the potential to kill him. After discussing his options, including discharge from aftercare, the team agreed that Oliver should enter outpatient treatment to help him gain a foothold in recovery and, if nothing else, at least make it to his retirement date. If he continued drinking while in outpatient treatment, we would discharge him from treatment, leaving Oliver to deal with the negative consequences at home, in the service, and to his health. Remember, discharge from treatment also meant discharge from military service because of the liability problems caused by untreated alcohol dependence.

Although he had 23 years of military service, Oliver was not eligible for retirement (usually at 20 years) because he had less than a year left on the commitment he made over seven years earlier. It was possible to get approval for Oliver to have his last six months waived, but the paperwork would take at least six months to process. Therefore, this was not an option. Moreover, his wife wanted the military to "fix" her husband before he retired; I guess she did not want to deal with his drinking any longer. This placed Oliver's employers in a dilemma. Because Oliver had a 23-year history of being a good trooper, they did not want to release him from the military without his pension. For these reasons, the treatment team decided to exhaust every possible option in order to give Oliver a chance to succeed.

The treatment team's decision, while well-meaning, caused a dilemma for the outpatient treatment program. The treatment team wanted to keep Oliver in the program, yet needed assurance that he would not jeopardize the treatment of other community members by half-heartedly participating. However, they admitted him into treatment when Oliver verbally committed to participate. Verbal commitments are often useless in substance abuse treatment. That is, Oliver demonstrated an ability to "play the game" by making himself appear superficially successful while privately struggling. He knew the correct words to say, but his behavior often demonstrated his true level of participation and commitment.

In cases such as Oliver, practitioners often recommend the drug antabuse (disulfiram) to help ensure abstinence. Antabuse causes people to become violently sick if they consume alcohol while taking the drug. This includes alcoholic drinks, the alcohol in cough syrup, pickle juice, and some baking products. Some clients must stop wearing cologne because it contains alcohol. Antabuse hinders certain liver enzymes that assist with alcohol degeneration. As a result, acetaldehyde accumulates in the blood, producing nausea, heart palpitations, vertigo, uneasiness, weakness, extreme confusion, extreme vomiting, and hyperventilation. Symptoms usually last from 30 minutes to a few hours. Unfortunately, even without the presence of alcohol, antabuse (disulfiram) can produce unwanted physical symptoms such as drowsiness, headaches, restlessness, fatigue, a metallic taste in the mouth, and impotence (*Physician's Desk Reference,* 1999). The negative side effects of this drug coupled with the client's inability to continue drinking often contributes to noncompliance (Mooney, Eisenberg, & Eisenberg, 1992). In Oliver's case, he agreed to take antabuse. However, he quit taking it almost immediately because of the negative side effects. His refusal to take antabuse ended in relapse.

By accident, I discovered Oliver's first known relapse during outpatient treatment. I personally caught him buying beer at a convenience store. While waiting in line to pay for a case of beer, Oliver saw me purchasing a soda and ice cream. Smiling, he said hello and then returned the case of beer to the shelf. I smiled, looked at the beer, and returned his greeting. To protect his confidentiality, I did not say anything more to him in the convenience store. Smelling like alcohol, he approached me in the parking lot and admitted to drinking "a few beers" that afternoon. In his next regularly scheduled session, he discussed the incident with a renewed commitment to abstinence. After a few additional incidents and multiple confrontations by other clients in the substance abuse program, he finally confessed to his team members and I that he did not want to abstain from alcohol. The bottom line here: Oliver was not prepared to admit that he had a problem with alcohol and was not committed to quitting.

Termination

Unfortunately, Oliver was not successful in treatment. He continued his abstinence and relapse cycle, refused to take antabuse, and found himself in trouble at work. He said that he was discontented with AA and refused to attend Rational Recovery. Because of his denial, or his refusal to change, he would not admit that alcohol was a big enough problem to warrant abstinence. When confronted about his refusal to engage, he gave vague reasons for wanting to continue drinking. Maybe he was not ready, maybe he had not "hit rock bottom," or maybe he had created such a complex matrix of deceptions and rationalizations that he was not capable of self-examination.

His refusal, coupled with increasingly worse relapses created an ethical dilemma for the substance abuse program and his work supervisors. If deemed a treatment failure, Oliver would be discharged early from the military and receive no retirement benefits. Only by serving the remainder of his time in the service alcohol-free could he receive full benefits. He struggled for another three months in the program. Finally, with three months remaining in his service career, his commander agreed to approve ninety-days of vacation. This "gift" helped Oliver reach his retirement date with pension—and his addiction—intact. After retirement, Oliver was transferred to the Veterans Affairs system and began civilian life. Despite the hard work of many practitioners, Oliver was unable to succeed in treatment.

Evaluation of Practice

The Aftermath

Evaluation of practice is an important component in social work. There are many facets to this process, one of which is reviewing themes and issues in clients' lives that played a role in their treatment. Critically reviewing one's work often helps improve skills and improve treatment in the future. In the aftermath of Oliver's case, I reassessed three issues related to human diversity that played an important role during the treatment process. The first pertained to his multicultural marriage, the second to the "culture of substance abuse," and the third to the "culture of helping professionals." These three dimensions influence many aspects of social work practice. In Oliver's case, they played a significant role in the outcome of his treatment.

Multicultural Marriage.   Oliver, an American-born male, was married to a woman from the Philippine Islands. Inherent in working with clients from nationalities or cultures other than the practitioner's is the need for sensitivity and understanding (Devore & Schlesinger, 1999) about potential worldview differences and how the differences may affect client engagement and treatment. Oliver's wife had lived in the United States for 16 years and spoke fluent English. Despite her apparent "westernization," her perspective about issues stemming from her culture-of-origin created barriers in treatment, making it difficult to engage her in the process. In her culture, defying one's husband was unacceptable. This led her to support Oliver's deception and denials, leading to what some call the enabling process during all stages of his treatment. Moreover, she did not understand why we would not simply "fix" her husband by making the negative consequences of his drinking disappear. She wanted us to teach him to drink more responsibly. Hence, she never understood or accepted the concept of abstinence as the cornerstone of successful treatment (Mooney, Eisenberg, & Eisenberg, 1992). Her inability to understand or accept this idea posed a barrier in treatment.

Questions

In the preceding discussion, the author surmised that cultural misunderstandings made it difficult to engage Oliver's wife in treatment in a productive manner. Because her culture required her to support Oliver, she became an enabler, contributing to Oliver's continued drinking. This presents an interesting issue.

Over the years, the term "enabler" has become a common label assigned, mostly, to the wife or female partner of a male alcoholic. It is an important part of role theory, often used to describe the roles members of chemically dependent families adopt for survival (Johnson, 2004). This particular role label helped lead to the formation of the Children of Alcoholics (COA) movement across the United States. Yet, some believe that the definition of enabler has slowly changed to imply that the mostly female role causes or is responsible for furthering her male partner's addiction. That is, some believe that the enabler is just as responsible for addictive behavior as the addict is.

1. Explore the definition of the term "enabler" in the substance abuse literature to determine its original meaning as it relates to alcoholic families. As part of this exploration, examine the literature published by the COA movement. Be sure to include information that supports and challenges the concept.

2. After completing your examination, construct a definition of "enabler" in terms of its function in families, role in the development and progression of chemical dependency, and its usefulness in substance abuse treatment. Make sure to place your definition in the context of gender. That is, how often are enablers defined as male versus female?

To what extent do people blame the enabler for the behavior of other members of their family?

Culture of Substance Abuse.   Common among substance abusers, Oliver's web of deception and lies permeated his clinical presentation. Originally, he presented mild depression, perhaps in response to his impending life changes. Perhaps his depression contributed to the two-month gap between our original interview and revealing his alcohol dependence. Yet, even after he "came clean," the deceptions continued. I believe that Oliver had no desire to stop drinking. He simply wanted the problems caused by drinking to go away, and continue drinking. We could not determine whether his deceptions and denial masked past feelings or indicated mental illness because he continued drinking. Chemical dependency casts doubt on the origin and/or existence of mental disorders. To be accurate, practitioners must assess clients for mental disorders after the use of substances ceases in order to know if additional disorders exist (APA, 2000). Many of the desired side effects of alcohol and other drugs mimic mental disorders (Johnson, 2004), and can easily lead to inaccurate diagnoses or coexisting mental disorders.

Culture of Professional Helping.   This issue pertains to the practitioner's desire to help, and the lengths some practitioners go to help. I believe that practitioners must decide to work only as hard as their clients do toward change. Periodically, practitioners must ask themselves questions such as, "who is working harder?" and, "who wants it more?" If the answer to these questions turns out to be anybody but the clients, then the prognosis for successful treatment is poor. Throughout the treatment process, it was apparent that Oliver's treatment team worked harder and desired success more than he did. I discuss this issue in the next section.

Questions

The preceding discussion is important. Practitioners often have different definitions of what it means to be a practitioner. Some maintain permanent boundaries between their clients and themselves, while others make themselves available to clients out of a sense of professional duty. In substance abuse, many practitioners believe that they will become an enabler if they extend themselves too far (i.e., calling clients who miss appointments, etc.), while others believe that this level of involvement demonstrates hopefulness and provides motivation.

1. Think about the preceding discussion in terms of best practice methods and the professional code of ethics. In this context, discuss your beliefs about this issue. What are the relevant factors that go into making a professional decision about how much one should make themselves available to clients?

2. From your experience, under what circumstances would you consider "working harder" than a client?

3. Defend your position by using information from the literature, practice wisdom, agency policy, the code of ethics, and/or the experience of other student-colleagues.

Ethical Issues

Oliver's case presented underlying ethical issues that affected the treatment team's decision making and my approach to his treatment. The first revolved around the issue of allowing Oliver to make decisions with potentially harmful consequences; the right to self-determination. The second issue involved Oliver's underlying resistance to treatment. The third issue pertained to the earlier discussion about professional boundaries and misplaced motivation in the helping process.

Each of the issues listed above pertain to the ethical concept of "first, do no harm." Balancing the act of helping and the right to self-determination with the potential for harm can be difficult to understand and manage. In practice, clients must be allowed to live out the consequences of their actions, forcing them to face their problems and determine the location of their own "rock bottom" (Mooney, Eisenberg, & Eisenberg, 1992). Sometimes, this means backing away and letting clients make decisions that practitioners know are harmful. Unless clients have this option, practitioners can actually enable clients and help them avoid changing. By allowing clients to hit rock bottom, clients often gain insight into their problems and increase their motivation to change. However, this sometimes means that practitioners have to stand by while their clients put themselves at risk. It is important to remember that adult clients have the right to make their own decisions, even if the decisions are unhealthy and potentially harmful. Therefore, consequences, either positive or negative, develop because of their decisions, not the practitioner's.

We further identified ethical concerns related to Oliver's resistance and denial. During the early stages of treatment, Oliver indicated that he had additional problems that he was not prepared to discuss. This could have meant a number of things (e.g., early childhood abuse, past traumas, substance abuse, etc.), but we did not know for sure what he meant. Once he revealed his alcohol dependence, we understood the incongruence between his problem presentation, behavior, and progress (or lack thereof) in treatment. However, we treated Oliver for depression for over two months before discovering that he really needed substance abuse treatment. For over two months, his problems went undiagnosed and untreated. This led us to reconsider the impact his denial and resistance had on our time, finite resources, the effects of an unmotivated client on the treatment of others, and the role we might have played in sustaining his problems.

I believe that it is important to "start where the client is" in treatment. Yet, in Oliver's case, at no time was he prepared to address his drinking. This fact remained consistent throughout his treatment at all stages and locations. Ethically, practitioners must be able to justify their actions regardless of outcome. In Oliver's case, although I worked with his employer to find positive options, I still question whether Oliver may have become more amenable to treatment if his employers and the treatment systems were not so flexible.

The final issue of misplaced motivation and professional boundaries also has ethical implications. At each step of the treatment process, Oliver resisted the idea that his drinking caused and/or exacerbated his other problems. Despite my best efforts, the efforts of two treatment programs, his physician, and employers, Oliver did not quit drinking. Almost daily, we stressed the importance of treatment, while Oliver paid "lip service" to their assertions and never accepted it as fact. When we put more effort into treatment than Oliver, was it time to question how much was enough.

Change is hard for many clients. While it is important for practitioners to support clients through the change process, people do not change their life unless they want to by making a concerted effort to reach their goal. In Oliver's case, he did not make that effort. Ethically, social workers must do everything in their power to help clients understand their responsibility to follow through on their commitment to take care of themselves. Our job is not to try to do it for them. Unfortunately, this was often the case with Oliver. Perhaps, the bigger issue is for practitioners to know when it is time to admit that treatment is not working.

Questions

The author forthrightly discussed issues that may have contributed to Oliver's unsuccessful treatment outcome. This demonstrates an honest attempt to learn from every case, in an effort not to repeat problems with future cases. Given the context of the discussion pertaining to ethics,

1. Can you locate any further ethical issues or challenges not discussed by the author? If so, what are the issues for consideration?

2. Prepare a plan of action designed to resolve the ethical conflicts as you see them in this case, as if you were the primary practitioner.

The Case Review Process

I used multidisciplinary team meetings and a peer review process to evaluate my decision-making process in Oliver's case. These practices are designed to ensure that I used best practice methods at all times during the case. Because of Oliver's resistant nature, I consulted with colleagues on multiple occasions. Originally, this occurred in multidisciplinary staff meetings. During the meetings, I discussed Oliver with other professionals for feedback and ideas. I believe that team meetings and peer review are excellent ways to check one's work, methods, opinions, and decisions. Once Oliver's alcohol dependence diagnosis was confirmed, the treatment team and the certified substance abuse counselors worked together to ensure the best treatment options for the client. By using these peer review systems, ethical issues were discussed and decision making became an inclusive process.

I also rely on the peer review of case records to check the progress of practice. In Oliver's case, professional peers frequently checked charting, diagnosis, and treatment planning events. This process unfolded in two ways. First, colleagues regularly reviewed Oliver's mental health record. Following our agency format, peer review ensured that his diagnosis was consistent with his symptoms and that treatment was consistent with his diagnosis. Second, peer review included periodic discussion of cases with peers in utilization management roles. Having the individual review helped to explain extraordinary and/or nontraditional steps in the treatment process and ensured that the level of care was consistent with Oliver's needs. Not all organizations utilize the peer review and/or utilization management process. However, in Oliver's case, it helped me get a different perspectiveon his assessment and treatment.

Questions

Now that Oliver's case is completed, it is your turn to consider his case in total. Using the information presented in this chapter and your responses to the questions posed throughout the case,

1. Present a comprehensive assessment and treatment plan for Oliver. Where your ideas and plans differ from the author's, provide theory and practice materials to defend your choices.

2. While one cannot predict how a plan would affect outcome before the fact, given the plan you developed above, what factors do you believe contributed to the outcome discussed by the author in this case? What steps would you take with clients presenting similarly to improve engagement, motivation, and commitment to treatment?

3. Discuss with student-colleagues cases you or they have worked with that presented similarly to Oliver. What strategies did they or you utilize in your work, what was the outcome of these strategies, and do strategies make a difference with a client as unmotivated as Oliver appeared to be?

Bibliography _____

American Psychiatric Association (2000). *Diagnostic and statistical manual of mental disorders* (4th ed., TR). Washington, DC: Author.
Barker, R. L. (1999). *The social work dictionary.* Washington, DC: NASW Press.
Beck, A. T. (1967). *Depression: Clinical, experimental and theoretical aspects.* New York: Hoeber. (Republished as *Depression: Causes and treatment.* Philadelphia: University of Pennsylvania Press, 1972).
Beck, A. T. (1988). *Love is never enough.* New York: Harper & Row.
Beck, A. T., Rush, A. J., Shaw, B. F., & Emery, G. (1979). *Cognitive therapy of depression.* New York: Gilford Press.
Burns, D. D. (1999). *The feeling good handbook.* New York: Penguin Books.
Devore, W., & Schlesinger, E. G. (1999). *Ethnic-sensitive social work practice* (5th ed.). Boston: Allyn and Bacon.
Edinburg, G. M., & Cottler, J. M. (1996). Managed care. In Beebe, L., Winchester, N. A., Pflieger, F., & Lowman, S. (eds.), *Encyclopedia of social work* (pp. 1635–1642). Washington, DC: NASW Press.

Granvold, D. K. (1994). *Cognitive and behavioral treatment: Methods and applications.* Pacific Grove, CA: Brooks/Cole.

Greenberger, D., & Padesky, C. A. (1995). *Mind over mood.* New York: Guilford Press.

Johnson, J. L. (2004). *Fundamentals of substance abuse practice.* Pacific Grove, CA: Brooks/Cole.

Markman, H., Stanley, S., & Blumeburg, S. L. (1994). *Fighting for your marriage: Positive steps for preventing divorce and preserving a lasting love.* San Fransisco: Jossey-Bass.

Medical Economics Company (1999). *Physician's desk reference* (53rd ed.). Montvale, NJ: Author.

Mooney, A. J., Eisenberg, A., & Eisenberg, H. (1992). *The recovery workbook.* New York: Workman Publishing Company.

Payne, M. S. (1997). *Modern social work theory* (2nd ed.). Chicago, IL: Lyceum Books, Inc.

Schuckit, M. A. (1995). *Drug and alcohol abuse: A clinical guide to diagnosis and treatment* (4th ed.). New York: Plenum Medical Book Company.

Shulman, L. (1999). *The skills of helping individuals, families, groups, and communities* (4th ed.). Itasca, IL: F. E. Peacock Publishers, Inc.

Smyth, N. J. (1996). Substance abuse: Direct practice. In Beebe, L., Winchester, N. A., Pflieger, F. & Lowman, S. (eds.), *Encyclopedia of social work* (pp. 2328–2338). Washington, DC: NASW Press.

Turner, F. J. (1996). Social work practice: Theoretical base. In Beebe, L., Winchester, N. A., Pflieger, F., & Lowman, S. (eds.), *Encyclopedia of social work* (pp. 2258–2265). Washington, DC: NASW Press.

Carrie

Kelly Ward

This case demonstrates substance abuse treatment that includes multi-systemic factors and their importance in substance abuse treatment. Carrie's case also demonstrates the complete treatment process, from the initial phase of treatment (assessment) through termination. As you will see, Carrie had significant problems and worked hard to improve her life after accepting her problems with alcohol and other drugs. Initially, Carrie sought treatment to please her husband. However, she quickly realized that she needed help, regardless of her husband's wishes. Within a relatively short time, Carrie embraced the challenges of directly confronting her substance abuse and family problems. With professional assistance, Carrie struggled with her problems and found personal success. My work with Carrie took place in a suburban New Jersey private practice and lasted nearly three years. By termination, Carrie had progressed through the early stages of recovery and was on her way to long-term sobriety.

This is Carrie's story.

Initial Interview

My clinical supervisor referred Carrie to me for a substance abuse assessment and outpatient treatment. She came to the attention of my supervisor through her husband who had been a client of my supervisor's at various times over the previous years. My supervisor stated that she suffered from problems with alcohol and other drugs and that her marriage was in trouble.

Carrie presented as a petite, 25-year-old, married, upper-class Caucasian female. She had long, light brown straight hair. Carrie was dressed appropriately for the climate outside and was clean and neat. I could see that she was an attractive woman, but her lifestyle had taken its toll on her appearance. During the first session, she was very quiet and withdrawn. Carrie said that she weighed 92 pounds. At 5'3" tall, she seemed thin and underweight. When dealing with cocaine use and abuse, a client's weight can be an important indicator of use. Since cocaine is a stimulant drug, it suppresses the user's appetite, often causing significant weight loss. Carrie was too thin for her size and bone structure.

She requested treatment for cocaine abuse after her husband threatened to report her to the Division of Youth and Family Services (DYFS), the Child Welfare Agency in New Jersey. He believed that she was unable to be an effective parent for their two children because of her alcohol and other drug use. While his threat was enough to motivate Carrie to seek help, I was never clear on the threat to call DYFS. Had he made the call, he would have immediately found himself under investigation for failure to protect his children. Perhaps, it was a hollow threat, designed simply to motivate his wife to seek help, or perhaps he was desperate.

Throughout the first interview, Carrie remained withdrawn and quiet. She rarely made direct eye contact and her voice was low, devoid of affect. She sat in the furthest seat from me and sunk back into it, almost as if she were trying to hide in plain sight. She showed little facial expression. When I asked about her health, Carrie stated that she was not feeling well. She went on to say that while she sought treatment for cocaine use, she wanted me to know that she did not have a cocaine problem and did not need to stop using. However, she further stated that she would consider quitting because of her husband's threats. She did not want to risk losing her children.

Since one of our purposes for meeting was to conduct a substance abuse assessment, I decided to inquire about Carrie's substance use history early in the first session. Carrie reported openly that she had snorted powder cocaine daily for over six months, along with occasional marijuana and alcohol use. Although freely admitting to her use, Carrie denied that she had problems with alcohol or marijuana. She also denied smoking crack cocaine and, because of her "fear of needles," did not inject cocaine either. Her primary route of administration was inhaling, or snorting cocaine into her nose. Quickly following her admission, she again repeated her earlier denial about having a cocaine problem. The psychological defense system called denial is one of the most common characteristics substance abusing clients present during treatment (Johnson, 2004). Usually, clients will not admit to having a problem with substance use, or they will minimize the extent of their use in an effort to demonstrate that they are in control of their use. Denial allows people to continue using substances while rationalizing that their problems have nothing to do with substance abuse (Johnson, 2004).

Carrie and her husband, Joe, had two children, a seven-year-old boy named Joe, Jr. (JJ), and a four-year-old girl named Rachel. Carrie married Joe when she discovered that she was pregnant during high school. Joe was presently 30 years old and worked in the family-owned construction company. The construction company did very well financially, providing Joe and Carrie with an excellent income that provided Carrie every tangible good or service that she desired.

The wealthy lifestyle she gained through marriage was quite different from her upbringing. Carrie grew up in a working class family that struggled financially. Joe provided her with a new and often exciting lifestyle. She freely admitted that part of her initial attraction to Joe was his financial status. She went on to describe her relationship with Joe as turbulent, but acknowledged that her options were limited since she did not finish high school. She had only worked one job in her life, as a cocktail server for a short time during a brief separation from Joe, six years earlier.

Carrie considered herself a good mother, despite her cocaine use. She reported that her alcohol and cocaine use never interfered with parenting because she used at night, after the children were asleep. She also admitted that she had never considered the potential consequences if one of her children became sick and needed her help. Fortunately, that had never happened. The thought of her not being sober enough to help her sick children upset her. She had not considered that her drug use could have brought harm to her children.

Going further, Carrie admitted several attempts to stop using on her own, to several occasions where she used more than she planned, to using alcohol and other drugs alone, and to gradually discovering that she needed to use more (increase her dosage) to get her usual effect. She also reported, "doing things" while under the influence that she regretted, such as having sex with her drug dealer in exchange for drugs. Carrie stated that she had last used cocaine two days earlier. Carrie said that she was feeling extremely moody and jittery. This indicated that Carrie might have been experiencing withdrawal symptoms from cocaine. Although she was in denial about the extent of her cocaine dependence, after we developed rapport and I assured her of confidentiality, Carrie offered personal substance use information freely. In turn, I was able to use this information to make a DSM-IV-TR (APA, 2000) diagnosis of cocaine dependence and offer professional help.

Despite her admissions and stated desire to quit using, Carrie remained confident that she did not have a substance abuse problem. It appeared that Carrie believed that she could prove to me that she was only a recreational user by answering my questions forthrightly. That is, if she answered honestly, she must not have a problem. It was also possible that Carrie based her opinion on the extent of her problem by comparing her use to others in her peer group. Carrie used with most of her friends and a few family members. It was possible that her peers used more, convincing herself that she would have a problem only when she used as much as they did. It was also possible that she shared the common misperception that people with drug or alcohol problems have to be a "skid-row bum." Carrie certainly did not fit that stereotype.

Initial Intervention: Attending to Carrie's Immediate Needs

As stated above, by the end of the first session it was clear to me that Carrie met the criteria for a diagnosis of cocaine dependence. The signs of physical withdrawal indicated that she could benefit from an inpatient detoxification program that included treatment for chemical dependency. I came to this conclusion based on the clinical indicators discussed during the first session, including the amount and frequency of her use. After Carrie agreed with my assessment and recommendation, she signed a release of information consent form so that I could contact her insurance company for approval of the referral and placement in treatment. To comply with federal confidentiality rules and regulations, which are quite strict for substance abuse clients, they must give written permission before practitioners can contact their insurance carriers for managed care approval.

Based on my diagnosis, Carrie easily satisfied her insurance company's requirements for inpatient detoxification followed by an inpatient treatment of not more than seven days. It is important to note that inpatient detoxification and treatment is expensive. Many insurance providers do not cover this level of treatment. Carrie was fortunate that her husband carried excellent health insurance. Other insurance plans might have denied her request for inpatient treatment, approved her to attend intensive outpatient treatment, or only outpatient treatment with social detoxification.

My experience with managed care is similar to many practitioners—difficult. As a treatment provider, when I believe someone needs an inpatient program, insurance or managed care companies require that I justify my reasoning. Even if my justification is sound, it is the managed care company's discretion to accept or reject my recommendation. If it is accepted, the managed care company decides length of stay and sometimes, even what provider the client can use. Managed care has dramatically changed the substance abuse treatment field. Over the last ten years, I have seen the number of approved days in inpatient treatment decline from nearly three weeks to less than ten days. Fifteen years ago, inpatient treatment lasted at least twenty-eight days. Third-party payers never questioned or challenged the practitioner's recommendation and coverage was relatively uniform across insurance companies. Today, each insurance company has different criteria. It becomes even more problematic when clients do not have private insurance coverage and must rely on public treatment funding. Public funding makes finding quality treatment with available space difficult indeed.

Questions

Carrie was indeed fortunate to have excellent health insurance coverage. She was able to find a bed quickly in a professional treatment program. Assume for a moment that your client did not have insurance, and relied on public treat-

ment funding. While your client qualified for inpatient treatment, there were no open beds available for six months. Based on this assumption,

1. What would your overall strategy be for your client?

2. What steps would you take with your client to help her achieve early abstinence?

3. How would you handle the problem that might be associated with withdrawal syndrome from cocaine dependence? Before you can effectively answer this question, explore the current practice literature to discover (1) Is cocaine physically addictive? (2) Based on the answer to this question, what are the characteristics of withdrawal syndrome for cocaine addiction? (3) What does the literature state are the most serious medical/psychological threats to someone in Carrie's condition?

4. The author chose inpatient treatment as her first option because of the threat of withdrawal syndrome. What does the current substance abuse treatment literature claim is the most effective level of primary treatment for people dependent on cocaine and alcohol?

Inpatient Treatment Experience

Carrie admitted herself for detoxification and inpatient treatment at a local hospital. Because she was from a family with financial means, Carrie, her husband, and her inpatient counselor decided that treatment would be most effective if she could stay for thirty days, instead of seven days. Her insurance paid for some of the treatment and her husband agreed to pay the remainder out-of-pocket. This is one of the advantages enjoyed by clients with financial means. Most clients could not afford this option. Therefore, Carrie would receive a complete, thirty-day course of treatment.

The inpatient treatment program derived its approach from the twelve-step philosophy of Alcoholics Anonymous (AA) and Narcotics Anonymous (NA). Many inpatient programs utilize this philosophy so that clients can easily assimilate into twelve-step support groups in their home community following treatment. The treatment program consisted of attending at least three inpatient groups per day, including psycho-educational, support, and clinical treatment groups that allowed Carrie to examine herself more intimately. Carrie also participated in weekly individual counseling and daily AA and/or NA meetings.

While she progressed nicely in treatment, one day I received a telephone call from Liz, Carrie's inpatient counselor. Liz reported that Carrie and Joe had engaged in a serious argument during the visiting hour following family counseling. After the argument, Carrie was considering not returning home following treatment. According to Liz, the argument began after Carrie refused to tell Joe "everything" that she did while using drugs. Liz called me in her attempt to assess Carrie's alternatives following treatment. During a three-way telephone conversation, Carrie acknowledged that Joe and she argued often. There had been instances of physical abuse prior to the birth of their first child, but none since. She reported that they frequently engaged in intense arguments, but enjoyed the process of "making up." That is, arguing seemed to infuse the couple with sexual tension. After passionate sex, the couple would begin the "argument—sex to make-up" cycle again. She then stated that while other people thought their relationship was difficult, she was used to it and did not worry about her physical safety. Besides, according to Carrie, she had nowhere else to live and she wanted to be near her children.

Discharge and Aftercare Planning

Near the end of her thirty days in the treatment, Carrie, Liz, and I agreed on a discharge and aftercare plan. Carrie decided to return home after treatment and continue weekly outpatient treatment with me. She also agreed to attend ninety AA or NA meetings in ninety days following discharge. It is normal to expect clients to attend 90 AA or NA meetings in the first ninety days following inpatient treatment. This has become standard aftercare practice for several reasons. First, support groups provide a daily support network during the days immediately following treatment when the chance of relapse is high. Second, support groups provide positive peer pressure to stay clean and people for clients to talk to when they find themselves nearing a relapse. Third, through AA and NA clients meet many people that role model a drug-free lifestyle. Fourth, AA and NA also provide a drug-free social outlet, providing clients something to do and a place to go everyday without alcohol and other drugs. Fifth, attending different meetings (women only, first-step only, gay and lesbian only, etc.) allow clients to decide which meetings meet their specific needs. Finally, clients can identify with the people attending the support groups. These people know what clients experience as they try to develop a sober lifestyle.

Other elements of Carrie's discharge plan included marital therapy with Joe (who agreed to attend). Joe also agreed to attend twelve-step meetings designed for spouses of the chemically dependent. Consistent with AA and NA philosophy, Carrie also agreed to make no major changes in her life during the first year of sobriety. Despite this agreement, Carrie doubted the future of her relationship with Joe.

Discharge plans provide clients with support while building on the treatment they received during inpatient treatment. This was true for Carrie. She had done well during inpatient treatment. If she followed her discharge plan, Carrie could accomplish her goals. Yet, recovery can be a difficult road to follow, even if someone had a good inpatient experience and was highly motivated. The return to daily life and relationships can be similar to crossing a mind field while blindfolded—there is a potential for relapse and/or personal crises with every step.

Questions

The inpatient program Carrie attended, similar to most inpatient substance abuse programs in the United States, strictly followed the disease model-based,

twelve-step approach of AA and NA. This includes the expectation that clients will attend ninety meetings in ninety days following inpatient treatment. While this approach is standard practice in the United States, it has many detractors. Therefore,

1. According to the substance abuse treatment literature, what are the major tenets of the disease model and the twelve-step approach?

2. What does the literature have to say about chemical dependency as a disease? Look at all sides of this issue by citing authors and research that both supports and disputes the idea of chemical dependency as a disease.

3. What does the treatment literature say about the effectiveness of substance abuse treatment based on the disease model? What does the literature say about AA and/or NA success rates? What does AA or NA's organizational literature claim?

4. What would you do if Carrie was your client and she told you that she was uncomfortable with the philosophies and practices of AA/NA? What other approaches are available to help chemically dependent clients? What does the treatment literature say about the success rates of these approaches?

Aftercare: Carrie Returns to Outpatient Treatment

Following discharge, Carrie returned home to live with Joe and their children. She immediately began attending weekly outpatient treatment in my office. On her first visit, Carrie appeared to have gained weight. She was by no means overweight, but looked much healthier than she had thirty days earlier. Moreover, her eyes were clear and focused and she seemed more alert and attentive. Now that she was drug-free, clear, and eating well, Carrie presented as a beautiful young woman. These observations indicated that Carrie was most likely not using alcohol or other drugs and was following her discharge plan. Practitioners can tell a lot about their client's progress in substance abuse treatment by noticing week-to-week changes in their physical appearance. When they are clean, clients will look clean. However, their personal grooming, hygiene, and countenance often changes dramatically immediately following a relapse. Good substance abuse practitioners always look for physical clues about how their clients are progressing, regardless of what they say during a session. Now that Carrie was drug and alcohol free, I could concentrate on engaging her in outpatient treatment.

Client Engagement

A practitioner's personal background, style, and approach play important roles in her ability to engage clients in treatment (Johnson, 2004). Therefore, to discuss client engagement, it is important for you to know something about me. While I was a seasoned substance abuse practitioner at the time, Carrie was my first case as an outpatient practitioner. My previous professional experience was in a locked, mentally ill chemical abuser (MICA) unit in a hospital and in a long-term residential substance abuse treatment facility (therapeutic community). In both of these agencies, I worked mostly with mandated clients and the lack of client motivation was a constant issue. The legal system mandated that most of our clients attend treatment in lieu of incarceration. While many of our clients were difficult and complex cases, I always had backup built-in to our process. Treatment was planned and performed by multidisciplinary teams that served a consulting and support function on a daily basis.

In my outpatient practice, I work mainly with voluntary clients who generally had a higher level of motivation to change. We have a busy practice, and everyone is a solo practitioner. Hence, my colleagues are usually too busy to discuss cases, meaning that I do not have built-in consultation and support. This was a dramatic change in the context of my practice.

While I was treating Carrie, I was also in the midst of an unexpected transition in my approach and treatment style. I was learning—sometimes the hard way—that my highly confrontational and direct approach, expected in inpatient treatment centers, was not always effective in outpatient private practice. For example, there were times that I pushed Carrie to consider issues that she was not ready or able to handle. If I were Carrie's counselor in an inpatient program, I could push her to the limit knowing that she would receive support from other residents and staff. However, in outpatient treatment that support did not exist. In fact, I was her primary support person in that setting. I had to learn timing, when to be supportive, and when to push. I had to learn what issues to address, when to address them, and to modify my approach to ensure client engagement and personal safety. Pertaining to client engagement, practitioners walk a tightrope between the need to confront, and the need to support.

For example, one day Carrie could not find a babysitter for her youngest child, so she brought her daughter to our session. During the session, Rachel began acting up, constantly interrupting Carrie and demanding attention. Carrie seemed unfazed by this, and did not take charge of her daughter's behavior or attitude. I decided it was appropriate to intervene. I stepped in and assigned Rachel a "time out," as if I was her mother. At first, my intervention shocked Carrie and Rachel. Then Rachel began crying. The situation flustered Carrie, and she quickly went to Rachel and took her out of the time out. In my best parental voice, I let Carrie know that her parenting style was the reason she had problems with her children and that this had to change. Carrie did not know how to react. She left the session frustrated and hurt. I, too, felt frustrated as well. However, when I later processed the exchange, I realized that my authoritative style was inappropriate in that setting, at that time, and with that client. I needed to find a different way to work with Carrie specifically, and with my clients in general.

Often, busy practitioners do not stop to analyze how and why they practice as they do. As I do that here, I realize that the reason cases succeed usually involves the process of client engagement. The same was true with Carrie. When she originally came for treatment, she was externally motivated (to please her husband) and did not believe she had a substance abuse problem. This is a common presentation for substance abuse clients. Yet, denial presents practitioners with a paradox. While it must be addressed early in treatment, denial is overcome in the context of a strong and trusting therapeutic relationship (Johnson, 2004).

Carrie began engaging in treatment during inpatient treatment. There, she was confronted about her denial and forced to look at herself and her behavior in the "mirror." Program staff conducted individual and family sessions, but primarily used group therapy. Carrie participated in groups comprised of clients in different stages of the program, including clients who had already recognized the extent of their addiction and its impact on themselves and others. Hence, they were ready and willing to confront Carrie's behavior and denial. Often, newly admitted clients listen more intently to peers than they do professional helpers. This is especially true in the earliest stages of treatment. Hence, Carrie became willing to admit the extent of her chemical dependency and its involvement in many of her other problems. She also learned the tenets of the disease model, which I used extensively with her during individual therapy. This all occurred before she entered aftercare with me as her therapist.

Therefore, when Carrie arrived in my office for her first post-inpatient care session, she was already invested in her recovery process. Moreover, she was also riding high on what recovering addicts call the "pink cloud." That is, newly abstinent clients often believe the world is a beautiful place and that life will become easier and better now that they are sober; they are floating through life on their pink cloud, seeing it through the proverbial "rose-colored" lenses. At this stage, it is unthinkable that life may become more difficult, replete with difficult decisions and changes. The pink cloud develops shortly after detoxification, when clients begin feeling physically and emotionally healthier then they have in a long time. Educating clients about the nature of this period and that it will likely "burst" at some point helps lessen the possibility of a relapse. Dealing effectively and pre-emptively with the pink cloud syndrome is a necessary component of early client engagement with substance abuse clients.

As I stated above, when Carrie appeared for therapy, she was ready to accept my help and participate in her treatment. My job, at least initially, was to build her level of motivation and courage to face the issues that were on her horizon. When we met prior to inpatient treatment, we focused entirely on her substance use and family dynamics as part of an assessment. While treatment began that day, the context was different than it was when she returned. Technically, her first session of aftercare was our second session together. However, we had to start the engagement process over, despite her apparent level of motivation. She had engaged in treatment with the staff and program of the inpatient hospital, not me. I had to redevelop rapport in hopes of learning about the issues involved with her chemical dependency and finding ways to maintain her involvement in recovery and deal with her personal life and future.

To facilitate this process, I used our first session to process her inpatient treatment. Since I previously worked in an inpatient setting, I could converse forthrightly about her experiences in treatment. I recommend that anyone interested in the substance abuse field work for a while in an inpatient or residential treatment setting. It helps practitioners engage clients when they can demonstrate that they understand the interesting dynamics of the inpatient treatment process, since many clients will enter aftercare following primary inpatient or residential treatment. My experience in these settings helped the engagement process with Carrie. She seemed to appreciate that I could ask questions about her treatment in an informed manner; I understood the expectations of the program, and the level of direct confrontation used in these programs.

Since a significant part of her aftercare plan was to attend support groups, Carrie wanted to learn about the local NA meetings. I anticipated this request and made a meeting list available to her. Explaining how to read the meeting book (which can be complicated for a beginner) was useful and seemed to instill confidence that I was knowledgeable about chemical dependency and other addictions. I also recommend that new practitioners take a class in chemical dependency and attend "open meetings" of the various self-help groups to learn about the process. This will prepare you to answer questions and deal with client concerns. My experience in this area allowed the trust-building process to begin with Carrie.

As our early work continued, I educated Carrie about addiction and the recovery process while advocating that she continue regular attendance at NA meetings. I used empathy, tempered with firm but gentle confrontation about specific behaviors such as Carrie being with her sister-in-law when she got high, serving alcohol at her son's birthday party, and skipping meetings because she was too tired. Traditional chemical dependency treatment is highly confrontational and brusque (i.e., "What the hell do you mean you missed a meeting?"). I learned to use firm but gentle confrontation in my work with Carrie (i.e., "You need to attend meetings because they are essential to the recovery process. What needs to happen so that you don't miss any more meetings? Can you commit to making the meetings from now on?"). Carrie appreciated this type of confrontation. It added to her engagement in the treatment process because she believed that I had her best interest at heart, and I did not act offensively toward her.

Like many in the field, I had to learn how to confront clients and be comfortable with the process. Confrontation can be uncomfortable, misused, or come across as harsh and inappropriate. Constructive confrontation must stem from the practitioner's concern and compassion for clients. This takes time and practice. In my experience, learning to confront client behavior is an essential component of my work. Readers should practice being firm and insistent without becoming harsh and demeaning. Seek feedback from colleagues and recognize that confrontation is an essential skill that may save your client's life (literally) by helping to stop a relapse and/or a potential overdose.

Questions

For decades, direct and harsh confrontation has been a hallmark of substance abuse treatment (Miller & Rollnick, 2002). As the author stated above, these practices remain a centerpiece of most programs based on the disease model, specifically pertaining to client denial (Johnson, 2004). In recent years, many authors have challenged this practice at the levels of theory, practice, and practice outcome (Miller & Rollnick, 2002). As students and future graduate level practitioners, this discussion is important. Therefore,

1. Examine the current literature to learn the reasons for direct confrontation, as well as the pros and cons of this practice. It might be helpful to interview substance abuse practitioners or visit local programs to learn their perspectives on the use of direct and harsh confrontation in practice. With your data gathering complete, what is your position on this practice, and how do you defend your position?

2. Engage in a classroom discussion/debate with peers to enhance your use of critical thought pertaining to this important theoretical and practice issue.

Self-Determination and Substance Abuse Treatment

This is an appropriate time to discuss the concept of self-determination in substance abuse treatment. As a social worker, I agree with the NASW Code of Professional Ethics (NASW, 2000) that requires social workers to respect the client's right to self-determination. That is, if substance abuse clients are going to relapse, according to this standard, I have little control over their behavior and should respect their decision to relapse and work with that instead of trying to control their choices and behaviors. However, I believe that substance abuse treatment is different and that practitioners must be more directive to be successful. I see it as my duty to warn clients when I see signs of relapse. I confront the thinking patterns that allow them to entertain the notion of their ability to control their substance use. To me, being directive means that I not wait for clients to reach their own conclusions and make their own choices before intervening. I always try to "raise their bottom" by letting clients know that their decisions may lead to harm, before they experience a problem and discover this for themselves. I let clients know that they have choices, but the choice to use substances will have negative consequences for them and their families. For example, my position on this responsibility is different from the type of self-determination I promote when clients are pregnant and wanting an abortion. I believe this decision is the client's decision. I would not discourage their decision or confront their thought process; the right to self-determination is sacred in the social work profession. However, I believe that substance abuse treatment is different and requires different responsibilities because of the potential for serious physical harm and death.

Questions

The author described how she applies the notion of a client's right to self-determination differently in substance abuse treatment. Since the NASW

Professional Code of Ethics (2000) is designed as value statements that must be considered in practice and not rigid rules and guidelines, each of us must make decisions that meet the spirit of the code. This can be complex because often, practice dilemmas and/or approaches apply to several ethical standards simultaneously. In this context,

1. What is your position on the author's application of the ethical standard regarding the right to self-determination? In your informed opinion, is substance abuse treatment different from other social work practice specialties, as the author believes? To answer these questions adequately and in an informed manner, you will need to research the code of ethics, the treatment literature, and the experiences of yourself and your peers as you develop a position.

2. When you have developed a position, take a broader approach by listing and discussing other tenets of the code of ethics that apply in this particular circumstance. Does this approach alter your original position on the issue?

3. This issue would make an interesting classroom discussion about the application of the code of ethics to professional practice.

As stated above, practitioners must also be aware of their personal style and values in practice. Pertaining specifically to Carrie, I had to be careful about my reaction to some of her decisions before and after her recovery began. Her choices in the area of sexual activity and parenting were difficult to accept. Yet, my mandate was to be available to her in an open and nonjudgmental way. The ability to separate one's personal values from those of clients takes time, experience, and good clinical supervision (Johnson, 2004). It also relies on the ability to understand and appreciate why people narrow their personal range of options or become limited in their choices. I had to learn that most people do the best they can, most of the time. I also had to be aware of the potential impact of my expectations that clients act quickly to change their lives. I have to fight my natural tendency of not understanding why it can take clients so long to change. It is important to recognize when my natural style may be useful and when it is not.

My ten years in the substance abuse field has helped me understand and appreciate the choices that clients make, including their choices to use drugs, and the way early recovery affects certain people. For example, when Carrie began taking what she heard in NA meetings literally, without understanding how it affected her life, I intervened to expose her literal thinking. When members of NA suggested that she should avoid the people, places, and things from her days of active use, Carrie took their advice literally. She no longer frequented places she liked, even family gatherings, or saw people she knew when she was using drugs, although they were her only friends and many were family members. She even went so far as to avoid streets with bars on them, and refusing to listen to rock and roll music, changing to country music.

Since I often use humor to build rapport, I joked about her new music tastes and was able to help Carrie see that avoiding streets with bars and not listening to the music she loved was an extreme reaction to the suggestion to avoid people, places, and things. Avoiding old people, places, and things does not mean she should *not* enter establishments that serve alcohol or that she should *not* play her favorite music or that she should *not* attend family gatherings. It means that she should be open to new relationships, activities, and habits in recovery and not remain locked into old patterns.

Human diversity also plays an important role in client engagement. Since Carrie and I were both Caucasian and practiced the same religious faith, I did not believe that diversity would cause issues in our professional relationship. We did differ by socioeconomic class and on certain personal values, but these differences caused few problems. Her parents lived in the region where I attended college. Therefore, I understood her family's conservative "Midwest" views and values. My ability to translate her parents' opinions helped our relationship develop in a productive manner. When class-based or value-based differences arose, I addressed the differences to determine the extent to which they could interfere with the professional relationship.

Client Life History Information

Now that Carrie was returning for outpatient treatment, I had the time and relationship with her to conduct more thorough data gathering and assessment. Ultimately, we used this information to develop a treatment plan that suited Carrie's needs. The following discussion provides in-depth information about Carrie, her family, and the issues we considered in treatment.

Carrie's Family-of-Origin

Carrie is the middle child in a family of three. Her parents and one of her sisters lived in the Midwest. Her other sister lived with her two children close by. Carrie reported that she generally "got along well" with her sister Lynn and that she occasionally used drugs with her in the past. As a youngster growing up, Carrie said that the sisters had experienced a significant amount of sibling rivalry that continued to the present. Carrie, along with her sisters, acted as if they had to compete for parental love and attention.

Growing up, family parties always involved alcohol and other drugs. A few of her uncles, her sister, and several cousins used drugs and drank heavily at family functions. This trend continued into the present. Since the family was originally from the New Jersey area, her parents would come home from the Midwest twice per year to visit, and these visits always involved raucous family parties. This presented a dilemma for Carrie, especially now that she was attempting to establish her recovery. The two annual visits were the only time she could see her parents, and they always involved substance use.

During the rest of the year, Carrie said that she had little contact or communication with her family, except her sister that lived in the area. Hence, as a family, they were disengaged (Minuchin, 1974). They did not communicate often or well. For example, despite telling her parents that she needed to stay away from parties where alcohol and other drugs were available, the family parties continued and her parents complained that she did not attend. If Carrie refused to attend the gatherings, her parents refused to see her. They were unwilling to visit Carrie's home. This bothered her immensely. She worried that unless she attended the parties, her children would not get to see their grandparents and she would not get to visit her family. Furthermore, Carrie had recently attempted to discuss her addiction and recovery with her parents, but they would not listen. According to Carrie, all that her parents could "hear" was Carrie blaming them for her problems. Carrie had a difficult relationship with her parents and extended family, made more difficult because of the family's use of alcohol and other drugs as the primary vehicle for interaction and communication. Family life, it seemed, revolved around parties that featured substance use and abuse.

Joe's Family-of-Origin

Joe's family-of-origin lived and worked locally. They owned and operated a successful construction company that provided an excellent income. Many members of Joe's family worked in the family business, and, since Joe was the only male child, he was training to take over the family business from his father. Thus, he worked long hours at his father's side.

Joe's parents had been divorced for many years. Because of his work, Joe was in daily contact with his father, but he rarely communicated with his mother. Although it appeared that Joe and his father argued frequently and did not always get along, their relationship solidified whenever there was an issue between Joe and Carrie. As expected, under these circumstances, Joe's father and the family always sided with Joe. This left Carrie angry, frustrated, and feeling unsupported and misunderstood. Carrie claimed that generally, she got along well with her in-laws and the rest of Joe's family. That is, until there were disagreements between Joe and her. Moreover, given the frequency their arguments and disagreements, I assumed that Carrie's relationship with her in-laws was troubled more often than it was friendly.

The secretary in the family business was like a family member. Her position allowed her to enmesh in personal family business. She reported incidents involving Carrie to me during treatment. She had my telephone phone number because she kept track of the personal finances, and began calling to tell me how she thought Carrie was "taking advantage of the family's generosity." I let her know that I could not speak with her about Carrie, that it was inappropriate for her to call me, and that she should stop worrying. Clearly, Carrie's relationship with her in-laws was tenuous at best. As long as she agreed with Joe and, by definition, the rest of his family, she felt accepted and liked. This sense of belonging changed dramatically, at least in Carrie's perception, whenever she disagreed. This fit the pattern established in her family-of-origin that to be accepted, one must go along. She had come to believe that she must abandon her voice and wishes to feel accepted by Joe's family.

Carrie's Marriage and Family

Carrie came into her marriage dependent on her husband. She never received her high school diploma and by her senior year in high school was using alcohol and other drugs regularly. While they were dating, Joe encouraged her to drop out of high school. This left her with little education, fewer job skills, and feeling incapable of contributing as a functioning adult. She needed Joe to provide for her. Carrie and Joe had dated "off and on" since she was 15 years old. When she was 16 years old, Carrie became pregnant with Joe's child. When she told her mother about the pregnancy, she insisted that Carrie get an abortion, which she did. Further, her mother told Carrie never to discuss the issue again with anyone. That night, Carrie remembers using alcohol and other drugs in an effort to forget about the abortion, resulting in her first alcoholic blackout (Carrie forgot what happened) that night.

Shortly after her 18th birthday, Carrie and Joe married when she became pregnant again. Almost immediately, she began feeling "tied down" by the marriage, and their pattern of intense and frequent arguments began. She reported a few incidents of physical abuse early in their marriage, but these stopped when she gave birth to their first child. At 19 years old, Carrie could not take the arguing any longer, so she separated from Joe. During the separation, she rented an apartment and worked as a cocktail server. Joe took care of JJ (their first child) when she worked. Carrie reiterated that they separated mainly because of the constant arguing. At some point, Joe promised to change and purchased an expensive home as a present for Carrie. With that, she returned to the marriage. Two years later, Carrie gave birth to her daughter. Although they were together, Carrie admitted that their marriage had not changed since her return after the separation. Things were the same as before, arguing almost daily. Their family pattern evolved into frequent arguments followed by Joe buying her expensive apology gifts.

Yet, their arguments benefited the marriage as well. Carrie reported that their sex life had always been "great." They developed a cycle over the years, whereby they would argue, and then make up by having sex. Arguing created sexual tension in the marriage. One day, Carrie heard that cocaine would enhance her sex life even more, so she tried it for the first time. As many people do, Carrie thoroughly enjoyed the experience and reported that she became dependent rather quickly. She stated that she had used marijuana and alcohol throughout the early years of the marriage, but they had not become a significant problem. However, cocaine was different. Soon, she was using grocery money to buy cocaine, buying low-quality food items so that she could account for the money. Occasionally, she slept with her cocaine dealer in exchange for drugs. Carrie hid her drugs around the house, even in the baby's diapers. Since she was the only person to change diapers, she knew that Joe would not find them there. In time, Joe began noticing that Carrie could not wake up in the morning to get their son off to school. He also noticed that she began losing weight, was withdrawn, and began initiating arguments, unusual behavior for Carrie. Soon, their arguing became more intense and her parenting skills worsened, ultimately leading to Joe's threat to call social services and Carrie's admission into treatment.

The lengths that people go to find and use drugs rarely surprises substance abuse practitioners. For the chemically dependent, finding, using, concealing their drugs, and convincing self and others that "life is good" becomes their mission. Chemical dependency becomes their primary reason for living—their vocation. Nothing, including abusive behavior toward themselves and others, is off-limits to addicts when it comes to participating in their addiction (Johnson, 2004). This was certainly true in Carrie's life.

Carrie and Joe had two children. Joe, Jr., was seven years old and Rachel was four years old. She reported that both children had behavior problems. Her son rarely went to bed before 11:00 p.m. and refused to eat dinner at the table. His teachers reported a lack of focus and difficulty getting along with peers. Rachel was in preschool every afternoon. She also had difficulties with bedtime, but the more serious problems occurred at home and in preschool. Rachel refused to accept or follow any adult direction, from her parents or preschool personnel. Carrie reported that Rachel was "completely out of control" and often fell asleep at night only when Carrie held her tightly to stop her tantrums.

While Carrie was in treatment, her sister-in-law (Maureen) moved into the house to care for the children. Maureen had no children and worked part-time in the family business. Carrie's father-in-law encouraged Maureen to continue living with them, even after Carrie returned from treatment. He said he wanted Maureen to stay so that Carrie could have extra help. However, Carrie suspected that the real reason was to get Maureen out of his house. Maureen had smoked marijuana and partied with Carrie in the past. In fact, they bought drugs from the same dealer. Carrie stated that Maureen respected her decision to quit and agreed not to keep any drugs or paraphernalia in the house.

Carrie's Sexual Activity

Carrie also revealed that she had been involved in a series of affairs over the years. Her intense interest and desire for sex predated her involvement with drugs. She reported being obsessed with sex—that she "couldn't live without it." While having multiple affairs and sex with her husband, Carrie would flirt with men in public and at NA meetings, looking for opportunities for anonymous sex. She reported that she was excited by the prospect of having sex in public places, for example, in active mall parking lots, public restrooms, behind buildings after NA meetings, and so on. She described the feeling of pursuing sex and having sex, the same way as she described the feeling of finding and using cocaine. It made her high.

As she continued talking about her sexual history and the role sex played in her life, I began to wonder whether Carrie had a co-occurring dependency, alcohol and other drugs and sex. As her story progressed, I became more convinced that Carrie was, in fact, a sex addict. I also began to wonder if her addiction to sex was her primary addiction. It was possible that her chemical dependency was a replacement addiction for sex. Perhaps sex was her primary "drug" of choice all along.

Multi-Systemic Assessment

Pertaining to my overall assessment of Carrie's life and multi-systemic environment, several important areas contributed to her situation during the time she was in treatment. They were: (1) her family-of-origin, (2) her current family system, and (3) the clash between her two communities. I discuss each below.

Family-of-Origin

Carrie was the middle child and felt a significant need to seek attention from her parents and others, common for middle children. It appeared that she began this behavior at an early age. She sought attention primarily through negative acting out (i.e., her substance abuse and sex/pregnancy). For example, while her teenage abortion was difficult, it also succeeded in placing her at the center of her mother's attention. Additionally, dropping out of school to get married accomplished the same benefit. It made her different from her sisters. Yet, when it came to her relationship and marriage, her parents rarely commented, yet they made it clear that they did not like Joe and did not believe she should be married. Finally, when she separated from Joe, her parents told her they thought it was good to get away from him. While she yearned for positive feedback from her parents about her recovery, she never received it. Carrie's parents felt as if she was blaming them for her troubles and refused to discuss it.

Current Family System

Carrie's current family consisted of Joe and their two children. However, we must also consider her father-in-law as part of this family because of his influence. Her current family also included Carrie's live-in sister-in-law and the secretary. Carrie stated that she had no privacy. Joe gave detailed accounts of their domestic problems to his father and the secretary, who often tried to play peacemakers by meddling into their personal business. While Carrie's family-of-origin was disengaged, Joe's was enmeshed (Minuchin, 1974).

Initially, Carrie enjoyed feeling that people cared for her and were looking out for her well-being. She liked being part of a close-knit family. However, the longer she was in recovery the more she became aware of the unhealthy lack of boundaries between Joe's family-of-origin and her family. She wanted more privacy and distance from what she believed was constant judgment by Joe's family and the secretary. In response to this need, Carrie sought distance and personal space, ultimately leading her into more extramarital affairs. Her affairs provided her a life separate from Joe and his family.

The children were also sources of havoc and stress. Because of her addiction, she had been unable to provide structure for the children. Although they were both young, imposing structure and discipline in order to develop respect for her authority was challenging. Her son was tested and diagnosed with Attention Deficit Hyperactive Disorder (ADHD). It appears as if her daughter might also have ADHD.

Two Communities

Carrie lived and interacted in two distinct communities: her affluent neighborhood and her NA community. She felt strangely out of place in her neighborhood. Because of Joe's income, they lived in an affluent neighborhood. Many of her neighbors commuted to New York to work on Wall Street or other executive business positions. Without the benefit of a completed high school education or GED, Carrie felt as if she did not belong and that her neighbors probably "looked down" on her. She rarely visited with the neighbors; trying to have little contact with them.

In contrast, Carrie loved her NA meetings. She volunteered to drive people to and from meetings and committed to being "greeter" at the meetings almost immediately. This responsibility meant that she had to arrive at meetings early to welcome new members, who usually feel uncertain about coming into a strange group of people for the first time. Soon, Carrie began to spend much of her time with this community. She felt accepted and understood for the first time in her life. Her sponsor and other contacts within the recovering community assisted and supported her growth process. They helped her learn the difference between being abstinent and living a new life in recovery. That is, developing a new lifestyle that did not include alcohol and other drugs, but also one that required her to change the fundamental way that she approached self and others. As one can imagine, Joe had trouble understanding why this community became so important. He also complained about the newfound independence that she was enjoying through her own support network.

We had to address the interacting issues stemming from Carrie's family-of-origin, family of creation, and the NA community in individual treatment. As you will see, while the majority of treatment focused on her recovery, each of these areas affected her recovery and potential for relapse. For example, if she continued to attend family barbecues, she might easily be encouraged to drink. If she did not change her relationship with Joe, she would continue to feel dependent, worthless, and seek solace in sexual encounters outside her marriage. This sense of personal dependency and her sexual coping mechanism could have easily driven her to relapse. Treating Carrie as if she were separate from the influence of these systems would have made our work incomplete and perhaps contributed to a relapse.

Questions

Using her chosen theoretical approach, the author provided a detailed account of Carrie's life, including her relationship with her extended family and in-laws. The author also presented a detailed look into Carrie and Joe's marriage,

and was comfortable making diagnoses and developing a treatment plan based on the information provided above. Prior to moving on to treatment planning and intervention planning, it is appropriate to ask that you respond to the following questions.

1. Based on your knowledge of Carrie's circumstances and before completing your final narrative assessment, is there any additional client information that you would want to ascertain? If so, what questions would you ask Carrie if you were able to meet with her face-to-face? Please be prepared to provide your rationale for needing further information.

2. What was the author's theoretical approach and what information does her approach require? Based on your learning, what other theoretical approaches may be used to engage and collect life information from substance abusing clients?

3. You have read the author's assessment of the case; now it is your turn. Based on the information provided, please write your narrative assessment that encompasses Carrie's multi-systemic life history. Does your assessment and diagnoses concur with the author's? If not, please defend your decisions with client data or by pointing out data that you believe is missing.

My Ethical Dilemma

My work with Carrie presented issues regarding the Code of Professional Ethics (NASW, 2000). In my judgment, the most significant ethical issues in this case involved client confidentiality and supervision. I discussed the issue pertaining to self-determination earlier. Here I discuss my ethical dilemma related to confidentiality and supervision. As stated earlier, my clinical supervisor referred Carrie to me for treatment. My supervisor had been Joe's therapist for years. When Carrie began treatment, Joe simultaneously elected to return to individual treatment. Hence, both spouses were in simultaneous individual treatment: Carrie with me, and Joe with my supervisor. My internal professional relationship with my clinical supervisor posed a dilemma related to confidentiality.

To protect Carrie, I decided that I could not discuss sensitive issues with my supervisor; particularly about Carrie's extramarital affairs, for fear that this information would accidentally find its way to Joe. Therefore, we confined our supervisory relationship to Carrie's recovery and parenting skills, making supervision less effective. I was reluctant to discuss Carrie's case in full. This raised two issues. First, I could not process my feelings and value conflicts with my supervisor. Second, I felt that I was lying by omission to my supervisor. I resolved this ethical dilemma by seeking outside supervision for my work with Carrie. Gratefully, my supervisor respected the boundaries I placed on our professional interactions and never asked my reasons for finding alternative supervision.

Question

Given the particulars of this case known to this point, can you find any additional potential ethical conflicts that must be resolved? If so, explain the conflicts and develop your plans for resolving each.

Treatment and Intervention Planning

Following the multi-systemic assessment discussed above, Carrie and I developed a reasonable treatment and intervention plan. This plan needed attainable goals and objectives and to be agreeable to Carrie. The following discussion pertains to the central issues considered in treatment and our plans for addressing them.

According to my assessment, Carrie presented with numerous issues: sexual addiction, chemical dependency, marital problems, grief and loss over her abortion, parenting issues, her relationship with her parents, and her educational deficits. Pertaining to intervention planning, our first goal was to help Carrie solidify herself in recovery from chemical dependency by encouraging NA attendance and helping her understand the recovery process. In addition to NA, we approached this goal by encouraging her participation in psycho-educational sessions and by following the disease model embodied by NA and her inpatient treatment program.

As it turned out, recovery was the easy part of Carrie's treatment. Dealing with the other issues was not so smooth. We consistently debated and discussed the best way to address her sexual addiction, marriage, grief over the abortion, parenting skills, and GED for several sessions. Carrie wanted to address her parenting skills, grief and loss, and her relationship with her parents while we worked on solidifying her recovery. However, she refused to address her marriage, denied her sexual addiction, and was intimidated by the prospect of pursuing her GED. Carrie feared that she lacked the structure and ability to succeed in school. While I believed it was important to address her sexual addiction, GED, and marriage because they could help strengthen her recovery by testing her coping skills, I followed her lead. I chose to focus on her recovery and allow Carrie to choose her own priorities.

I primarily treated Carrie in individual therapy. Since she had participated in groups during her inpatient treatment and attended NA meetings almost daily, group work seemed contraindicated. Because she benefited from her group involvement in NA, we decided that she would benefit more from individual treatment, giving her time to explore her issues in private. We planned to use family and couples counseling, but this never materialized. Carrie steadfastly resisted marital counseling and because the marriage was so chaotic, we decided to omit this effort from our treatment plans. I believe that discussing the prospect of relationship therapy with clients and gauging their response allows practitioners to determine how clients feel about entering couples therapy. Carrie did not want to tell her husband the things that he insisted on knowing—primarily about her sex life. She believed these revelations would harm the marriage more and not be useful. Yet, she did not want to lie either. Hence, if they did not have marital therapy, she would not have to reveal her activities or lie. She could simply ignore him. Therefore, Carrie refused to attend therapy with her husband. We tried to have Carrie's parents join her treatment while they were in town, but were not able to make their schedules mesh.

Question

The author believed that Carrie and Joe could benefit from marital counseling, but decided against it for a variety of reasons, most notably Carrie's resistance to the idea. If you were Carrie's therapist and you believed strongly, as the author did, that marital therapy was indicated, what would you do to encourage participation by both partners? Would you handle this case similarly to the author, or would you take a different approach? Please explain.

Progression of Treatment

Over the nearly three years of her treatment, Carrie made steady progress toward her goals. Once she began following the NA program, she recognized and understood that she was chemically dependent. With this realization, through our treatment and support from NA, she made dramatic personal changes. In NA, the criterion for membership is the desire to stop using substances. Hence, everyone on the program is in recovery or trying to find a way to become abstinent. Group members, not professional helpers, facilitate meetings focused on various aspects of addiction including how substances affect people's lives and how to stay sober—one day at a time, using the twelve-step framework. This structure of support and belonging motivated Carrie to seek and maintain recovery. She attended the ninety meetings in ninety days she agreed to in her discharge plan, found a sponsor, and never missed a counseling session. In treatment, Carrie worked to express grief over her abortion, identify and express emotions, find an outside interest to fill her time, return to school for her GED, improve communication with her husband, and develop her parenting skills.

Accepting Sexual Addiction

Eventually, Carrie admitted to a sexual addiction and became willing to work on this issue. She changed her mind about the nature of her desire for sex after a one-night stand with a man in NA. She regretted her actions and that the affair had cost her the man's friendship. Simultaneously, her NA sponsor confronted her for crossing over to the "13th Step." AA and NA consider people who have sexual relationships with other members to be practicing the 13th step. The program discourages intimate relationships between members during their first year of sobriety because of the potential for troubles and tensions within the group and for contributing to the potential for relapse.

About one year into her recovery, Carrie revealed to me that she had recently bumped into a man with whom she had an affair five years earlier. Carrie believed that this was the man for her and contemplated calling him. Then, coincidentally, she bumped into him again at a local restaurant and they rekindled their affair. Getting her to recognize that this affair was a replacement addiction took a long time. After five months, she agreed to stop the affair and began applying the twelve-step approach to her sexual desires. Yet, Carrie continued to have numerous sexual encounters while maintaining sexual relations with her husband. It was apparent to me that Carrie was in relapse, but not with drugs. We concluded that alcohol and other drugs were her replacement addiction. Sex had been her primary "drug" of choice all along.

We spent most of the following year talking about her desire for sex and the personal needs it fulfilled beyond the obvious. As part of her treatment, Carrie agreed to be abstinent from sexual activity and established behavioral guidelines. We agreed that she could have sexual relations only with her husband, in her house, and no more than four times per week. Carrie agreed to the guidelines. She continued to attend NA meetings where she felt comfortable rather than Sex Anonymous (SA) meetings.

Questions

Considering sexual addiction, along with other process addictions (i.e., gambling, eating, exercise, etc.) as addictive diseases is more widely accepted than ever before. However, this is controversial. That is, not only is the existence of process addictions controversial, so is the idea of any addiction being called a disease (Johnson, 2004). Therefore,

1. Using the professional literature, what evidence exists pertaining to the issue of process addictions as treatable diseases? Based on this evidence, what is your position on this issue?

2. Similarly, what does the latest evidence say about addiction as a disease? Based on this evidence, what is you position on this issue.

3. Based on your answers to the previous questions, what are the implications for practice contained in your findings?

Marital Problems and Big Decisions

At the same time, Carrie began feeling increasingly unsettled in her marriage while Joe grew increasingly intolerant of her NA involvement. This is a common occurrence in relationships where one person is newly recovering. Many spouses do not appreciate the commitment their partners must make to remain sober. Having just lived through chemical dependency where their partner was obsessed with drugs and using, they now live with their apparent "obsession" with recovery. Many spouses do not see the difference, and it causes significant problems in relationships.

The people she became friendly with in the program also bothered Joe. In NA, Carrie met people from diverse backgrounds and lifestyles including ex-convicts, the poor, gays and lesbians, and people of color. She easily accepted this diversity, but sometimes found it difficult to understand how someone could lack transportation or have logistical or personal problems that prevented them from holding a job. We were able to discuss and process these issues during individual treatment.

Meanwhile, her friendships in NA became a significant problem for Joe, and their marriage. He was not open to diverse lifestyles. He did not want Carrie to invite her NA friends to their home. Joe hoped that his refusal would end the relationships. Instead, it alienated Carrie further from him and their marriage. If she wanted to see her NA friends, Carrie had to leave the house. Much to Joe's surprise and disgust, this is exactly what she did almost daily. He did not count on her interest in her new friends to be so strong, nor did he expect to lose his "control" over her as she progressed in her recovery. She was becoming more independent, needing Joe less to control her life and arrange her activities. According to Carrie, Joe's intolerance of NA and refusal to see that it was important to her recovery created undue stress in the household.

Moreover, after just two visits, Joe refused to continue individual therapy with my supervisor and to take the psychiatric medication prescribed for his anxiety. As stated earlier, neither Carrie nor Joe was interested in marriage counseling. Hence, the marriage was crumbling. To Carrie's credit, despite the pressures, she followed her recovery program and celebrated two years' sobriety. Shortly thereafter, she left the marriage.

This presented serious challenges. Carrie had no health insurance, no job skills, no GED, and was unemployed. To be successful, Carrie had a lot of planning to do. She enlisted the aid of her NA sponsor who helped her find a job and a place to live. In the midst of her planning, Joe found out about her plan and reacted by destroying her clothes, taking her jewelry, and selling her car. This left Carrie without many resources. Yet, she was different. In the past, Carrie would have responded by staying in the marriage as a way of reclaiming her "things." Despite Joe's efforts, Carrie chose to leave the marriage and strike out on her own.

Questions

Above, the author discussed a common occurrence in substance abuse treatment. The nonaddicted spouse or partner often begins resenting their partner's involvement in their chosen recovery program. In fact, there is some statistical evidence that more couples divorce after sobriety than during active addiction (Johnson, 2004). Given the prevalence of this as an issue,

1. What are the central issues that contribute to this as a significant problem in substance abuse treatment and recovery?

2. What would you do as a substance abuse practitioner to address this issue?

Termination/Outcome and Follow-Up

Termination is a critical component of social work practice and begins the moment clients enter treatment. Our goal as social workers is to help clients develop coping skills and strengths that allow them to make positive changes based on their own informed decision-making process. Hence, there are several issues of concern when considering termination. First, it is important to recognize client growth, reinforce their sense of self-efficacy, and develop a list of issues they will need to continue working on in their life. Second, it is also important to discuss the therapeutic relationship and the role it plays in the recovery process. Often, because of the chaos in their lives, clients have many people that come and go, but rarely have the opportunity to put closure on a relationship. The termination phase of practice provides that opportunity.

Because her husband cut her off financially, for a short time after her separation, Carrie continued therapy at a reduced rate. However, between needing to work full-time, NA meetings, and caring for her children, it became difficult for her to remain in counseling. We spent several weeks discussing her need to leave treatment and the issues she needed to continue addressing. We discussed the changes she had made in treatment and acknowledged that she had resolved many of the issues she entered with or that arose during treatment. She still needed to develop employment skills and pursue her GED.

We talked about my role in her life in the future. The possibility loomed of a custody battle and we discussed my ability to testify on her behalf. Although I was willing to testify, I informed her that permission to testify would provide access to personal information that might not be beneficial to her case. She stated that she would let her attorney make that decision. With that, we successfully terminated Carrie from treatment.

About eight months after termination, Carrie contacted me and asked for my support in a custody hearing. I provided the court a letter that detailed her treatment issues and described her growth. Carrie had also wanted me to attend court with her for support. After we discussed this option, she decided that I should not attend; she worried that my presence might cause trouble for her during the legal case.

Evaluation of Practice

To treat Carrie, I used a disease-based, twelve-step model and cognitive behavioral therapy that relied on changing behavior through altering her thought processes. I believed that Carrie needed to examine her issues from different perspectives and that she would benefit by understanding how her therapy, NA membership, and family life affected her behavior and decision-making process. We explored her thought processes and developed a thorough plan that allowed Carrie to change her behavior after changing the way she perceived herself and her world.

We measured Carrie's progress by tracking her accomplishments related to her treatment plan. When treatment began, Carrie focused on staying sober and understanding the recovery process. Family goals included her parenting style and addressing relationship problems she was having with her parents and her husband. Individually, we wanted to address sexual behavior, help her find training for a job, get a GED, and deal with the grief and loss related to her abortion.

Carrie remained sober and did not relapse on substances during treatment. She became a more effective parent by providing structure and discipline for her children. Her marriage ended, but this turned out to be positive. It forced her to examine her relationships. Through this process, Carrie realized that her marriage was unhealthy and was a significant part of her dependencies on substances and sex. She continued to visit her parents occasionally and they grew to respect her decision to avoid family gatherings that involved alcohol. In time, she grew strong enough in her recovery to be around people who were drinking and not feel the urge to drink with them. Then, she was able to attend family functions.

Carrie showed progress in the depths of her insight about herself and her decision making. Her emotional growth, along with the openness to recognize and address her sex addiction, was important to her future. She eventually earned her GED. Carrie addressed her grief and loss stemming from her abortion and began to understand and appreciate her mother's decision about the abortion. In the end, Carrie was happy that her mother forced her into that choice at that time in her life.

Overall, treatment was successful. I would have liked marital and family therapy integrated into Carrie's treatment plan. This may have provided a clearer picture about her family issues. Yet, overall Carrie made tremendous personal progress. She continues to do well in life, recently celebrating her eighth year of sobriety. She recently called to tell me of her plans to remarry.

Questions

Now that you have finished reading and studying this case, you get the chance to express your opinion about the overall approach and practice methods the author used with Carrie.

1. Overall, what is your immediate clinical opinion about the approach the author used with Carrie? Please explain and defend your opinion using existing literature, practice experience, and with input from student-colleagues.

2. Overall, what would you do differently if you met "Carrie"?

3. While it is difficult to argue with a successful outcome, what differences do think would occur if you were treating Carrie based on your persona, style, approaches, and/or clinical preferences?

4. When examining the author's approach to termination, are there additional issues that must be addressed during the termination phase of treatment? If so, what are they?

5. When examining the author's approach to practice evaluation, are there additional steps that could be implemented that would improve your ability to evaluate clinical process and outcome? What are they and why would these steps be important?

Bibliography

American Psychiatric Association (2000). *Diagnostic and statistical manual of mental disorders* (4th ed., TR). Washington, DC: Author.

Johnson, J. L. (2004). *Fundamentals of substance abuse practice.* Pacific Grove, CA: Brooks/Cole.

Miller, W. R., & Rollnick, S. (2002). *Motivational interviewing: Preparing people to change addictive behavior* (2nd ed.). New York: Guilford Press.

Minuchin, S. (1974). *Families and family therapy.* Cambridge, MA: Harvard University Press.

National Association of Social Workers (2000). *Code of ethics of the National Association of Social Workers.* Washington, DC: Author.

4

Frank

Jerry L. Johnson

A colleague referred Frank to me for substance abuse outpatient treatment after Richard, my colleague, could not engage Frank in a therapeutic relationship. Richard only met with Frank once and said that Frank and he were "not a good fit." Richard believed that I would be able to engage Frank in treatment. Since the early days of my career, I have worked diligently to develop the ability to engage "difficult" clients. Frank and I met early in my practice career and while I wasn't yet the most skilled technical clinician, I could engage difficult clients. I have always enjoyed a challenge; I suppose a by-product of my early years as an athlete. Besides, I knew I would have excellent supervision and case consultation available from Richard every step of the way. Knowing that I had support made tackling this challenging case more appealing. Frank's case certainly qualified as "challenging."

Let me explain.

Frank's Situation at Referral

All that I knew about Frank prior to our first meeting was that he was a 33-year-old African American male who had been arrested for shooting his wife of seven years. Richard claimed that Frank was awoken by his wife and "came up shooting" from a deep sleep. Richard did not know how Frank found a gun so quickly, at that late hour. His twin toddler daughters were not involved in the incident. He had previously been arrested three times for drunken driving, the most recent being six months earlier. He remained on probation for his last drunken driving offense and was yet to be adjudicated for the shooting episode.

When he made the referral, Richard reported Frank's history of drinking to intoxication. He also reminded me that Frank was especially at-risk for problems resulting from his drinking and driving because he was a long-haul trucker. Frank sought treatment, according to Richard, at the behest of his attorney in hopes of limiting the punishment that was sure to come because of the shooting. Frank's only interest, according to Richard, was to influence the judge. He had no other personal stake in seeking help.

Questions

1. Given what you know about Frank and his current situation, what issues would you consider as you prepared to meet him for the first time?

2. Since client engagement seemed to be a problem for Richard, how would you prepare yourself to overcome the issues that Richard described?

3. Before reading the next section, how do you approach involuntary clients in your practice?

Working with Involuntary Clients

Frank is what practitioners refer to as an "involuntary" client. He sought help under external duress (Murdach, 1980) after behaving in ways considered troublesome to society (Cingolani, 1984). Frank's status and presentation differed from so-called voluntary clients who "choose" to seek and, theoretically, accept help (Rooney, 1992). Frank hoped to beat a pending court case. In the beginning, the court case motivated Frank to attend therapy, not the need to make personal changes. Involuntary clients are the source of much disdain in the helping professions because they can be difficult to engage in treatment. Yet, I believe that problems with involuntary clients relate more to the artificial dichotomy (voluntary versus involuntary) than to the person of the client and how they decided to attend therapy.

According to social psychologists Thibaut and Kelley (1959), an involuntary relationship between helper and client contains at least one of the following elements. First, clients must feel forced to remain in the relationship because of physical or legal mandate. Second, they may choose to remain in an involuntary helping relationship because the cost of leaving is too high, and/or third, clients believe that they are disadvantaged in the helping relationship because better alternatives are available and they cannot benefit because of the involuntary relationship. Accordingly, Rooney (2002, 1992) subdivides involuntary clients into two subgroups: mandated and nonvoluntary clients. According to Rooney (1992), clients are defined as mandated if they "must work with a practitioner as a result of a legal mandate or court order" (pp. 4–5). Nonvoluntary clients enter into a relationship with a helping professional because of "pressure from agencies, other people, and outside events" (p. 5).

Rooney omits an important definition, what constitutes a "voluntary" client. Hence, an important question remains unasked and, therefore, unanswered. I agree with Rooney's (1992) central thesis that most social work education and training focuses on work with so-called voluntary clients, and that little occurs to prepare practitioners for the inevitability of spending much of their professional practice career with clients coerced into treatment by personal issues, persons, agencies, or legal authorities. Social work education and training assumes that most clients are ready, willing, and able to participate in their own treatment (Rooney, 2002). Hence, professional social work education may be out of touch with the real experience of daily practice.

Questions

1. Think back over your educational career. What training or education have you received that specifically prepares you to work with involuntary or coerced clients?

2. What strategies have you learned or practiced that specifically address working with involuntary or coerced clients?

3. What is your attitude about clients involved with the legal system, and what factors contribute to this attitude? Where did this information come from: practice experience, personal bias, instructor bias, or some other place? Do coerced clients deserve the same consideration as other clients, or have they given up their rights because of their "offender" status? Present evidence from the professional literature to defend your position on this issue.

After more than 20 years of practice experience, I have seen few, if any, truly voluntary clients. While there are exceptions (a few people with the time and resources to enter therapy simply to understand their existential place in the world), the vast majority of clients, even in private practice, seek help under coercion. This may be pressure from an outside source such as friends, relatives, or employers or from internal pressures, usually combined with feedback from their environment. Internal coercion usually results from the belief (real or perceived) that people's lives are not going well, or that they are not happy or healthy, individually or in their interpersonal relationships. In other words, rarely have I met a client who, upon awaking in the morning, proclaimed his happiness and then decided to seek therapy! Something or someone forces most people to seek help; a choice they would not otherwise make.

Therefore, it follows that most clients—regardless of practice setting or problems—will resist help, at least initially. Rooney (1992) defines resistance as a constellation of client behaviors that include "provocation, intellectualization, projection, verbosity, seduction, withdrawal, passive compliance, martyrdom, flight from the scene, refusal to answer, lateness for appointments, and changing the subject" (p. 125). With coerced clients, resistance should be expected—considered the normal state of affairs and not an odd circumstance that automatically points to evidence of individual pathology. Yet, in the helping professions, resistance is a pejorative label for clients who oppose what practitioners believe is in their best interest. According to Rooney (1992), "resistance is a label assigned by practitioners to clients who have not acted to the practitioner's satisfaction" (p. 125).

I recommend that practitioners consider client resistance or ambivalence (Miller & Rollnick, 2002; Connors, Donovan, & DiClemente, 2001) as a normal and expected part of the helping relationship, what I call the "dilemma of change" (Johnson, 2004, p. 124). The following passage exemplifies the dilemma of change (Johnson, 2004):

> Consider, if you will, the following definition: a dilemma occurs when a person is presented with two or more options, neither of which appears good. In this light, your client's hesitancy to change is understandable. Clients often say, "My life may be difficult now, but what if I go through all that work to change and my life is still miserable? At least now I'm high and don't worry about life much." This remark is not a function of resistance or denial, but an accurate appraisal of a real possibility. Clients are not eager to change, nor is it certain that they will reap the benefits from achieving sobriety. In fact, many recovering substance abusers have said that it took a significant period of abstinence, sometimes years, before their lives became better. For some, this improvement never happens. People do not change without pain (guilt, shame, embarrassment), struggle (multiple relapses), and/or without considering a permanent return to their previous life ("It wasn't that bad . . . I had some great times on cocaine"). (pp. 124–125)

Pertaining to Frank, I intended to approach him the same as I approach every client, regardless of the circumstances of their referral. I work to develop rapport while seeking to understand Frank in the context of his life, history, issues, and strengths as part of the process of establishing a therapeutic relationship based on mutual trust and agreeable goals (Johnson, 2004). Early on, I do not challenge or confront, but ask questions, listen, and try to understand. Any label (resistant client) that satisfies my need or desire for comfort, ease, or control has no place in the therapeutic context.

Our First Meeting

Frank arrived about 15 minutes late for his first scheduled individual session in my office. Focusing on the need to build rapport, I presented myself as upbeat and encouraging, while looking for a topic of conversation to ease our way into the session. Practitioners often downplay the importance of social conversation as a prelude to clinical work. Yet, it is a critical component of successful client engagement. Our profession's title contains two words: social and work. Hence, there can be no "work," unless client contact begins with the "social" (Johnson, 2004). In my practice, rapport relates to the level of comfort clients feel with me, beginning with the initial telephone contact and proceeding through the initial social conversation in the first moments of personal contact. Rapport is built quickly (Glicken, 2004), while engagement takes longer. However, without rapport there can be no engagement. Therefore, I try to position myself so that an already anxious and suspicious client could relax as quickly as possible. Accordingly, I did not mention that Frank was late for the session, but simply welcomed him in a friendly and casual manner.

Questions

1. How do you handle clients who are late for sessions? Please explain yourself.

2. Before moving ahead with the case, consider the issues involved with client rapport and engagement. What is your approach to this issue, and to what importance do you give professional relationship building?

3. What are the most important factors in client engagement?

4. What percentage of your time do you spend working on and/or practicing your engagement skills? List several ways that you can improve or practice engagement skills.

Frank was a thin, tall man of African American descent. He appeared tired and worn, as if he was living a difficult life. He appeared much older than his stated age of 33. He was casually dressed in relatively clean blue jeans and a button-down flannel shirt. He was wearing a tattered cowboy hat that he quickly removed upon entering my office. His cowboy boots were, however, beautiful. Now, I'm not one to admire (or own) cowboy boots, but Frank's boots were what even I would consider attractive footwear. They shined and glinted in the light of the office. Almost the color of clean beach sand, they were adorned with what appeared to be hand-carved designs and some kind of ornate stones mounted around the ankle and down the top of the foot bed. Clearly, Frank liked his boots; and even more clearly, admiring his boots was a great place to begin rapport-building!

"Man . . . those are some nice boots you're wearing," I stated in an honest expression of admiration for his unusual footwear. "Where'd they come from?"

He looked down at his boots and extended his legs slightly in front of his chair so he could see them, almost as if he were looking at them for the first time. With a big smile and a hint of surprise in his eyes, he thanked me for noticing. "Not many folks like cowboy boots these days," he said. He then explained that he bought the boots while traveling over the road as a long-haul truck driver. They were made of snakeskin and hand tooled by a Native American artisan in South Dakota. The boots were Frank's "pride and joy."

This exchange led directly to a conversation about his work. There was plenty of time to get to other issues later. In relationship building, it is important that client interviews not become overly structured. Learning to work in a relatively unstructured format is how I operationalize the well-used social work phrase, "start where the client is." That is, once clients begin talking about themselves—regardless of what they are talking about—follow the conversation and do not direct it. Never rush into so-called clinical issues. Everything clients say about themselves, including comments about their cowboy boots, is a valuable part of the engagement, assessment, and later, the treatment process (Johnson, 2004). As it turned out, this seemingly casual conversation about cowboy boots and long-haul trucking became, as I would learn later, the most informative and important conversation we would have. I learned several important clues into Frank's world that would prove to be the key to understanding and treating Frank later. He was about to reveal information about himself, his life, history, belief systems, while placing his "private troubles" in the context of "public issues" (Mills, 1959, p. 2). Had I not asked about his boots, I question when we would have gotten to the information in a way that made contextual sense.

Frank had been driving trucks as an independent contractor for approximately nine years. Truck driving was his sole employment since his discharge from the military eleven years earlier. He said that he enjoyed the "privacy and solitude" that came with his profession. When alone, out on the road, he was free from pressure and worry, alone with his thoughts and memories—free to do his best to relax. He said that he craved the road and the sense of internal comfort it allowed him. He worried about his wife and two children, but also relished not having to be in the center of the "chaos" that he said goes with having twin toddler daughters. Most days, Frank found it difficult to ease his worries and fears—what he calls his "traveling partners." According to Frank, traveling alone over the road made his "partners" easier to manage.

The conversation segued from his internal "partners" to his human partners. Frank prided himself on being a family man. He married Fiona, a 28-year-old Korean-born woman who he met shortly after his discharge from the Army, seven years earlier. He described their marriage as "good," sighting the "normal" problems associated with marriage in general and with being in a cross-cultural marriage in specific. When asked what he meant by his last statement, Frank said that both extended families raised serious objections to the marriage originally. While his family had come to accept Fiona as part of the family, his in-laws did not accept him. Their twin daughters were born two years earlier. He thought having grandchildren would make Fiona's family "come around," but it had not.

Since he had mentioned military service, I asked him to discuss his service experience. Frank served two tours of combat duty in the Army during the Vietnam War. He was drafted out of high school and reenlisted for a second tour. When asked why he extended his tour, since most Vietnam veterans I knew couldn't wait to get home, he explained that his first tour was "OK." He claimed that he had nothing to "rush home" for, and his first tour had been uneventful so he signed on for a second. According to Frank, he had "pushed his luck" by reenlisting because the second tour was "different" from the first. While saying this, his body language and affect changed dramatically, from open and forthcoming to closed, dark, and flat.

Because this conversation occurred early in our first session, I decided to back off and leave his life story there for a moment. I did not want to risk driving him away by pushing into intimate or painful territory before having the relationship basis for such a push. I always work from the premise that sometimes, depending on the client; the best outcome of a first session is to build rapport in an effort to have a second session (Johnson, 2004). Pushing too hard or too quickly before a relationship develops often leads to inaccurate personal information and reduces the chance for a second interview. Despite my reluctance to proceed, his time in

Vietnam along with his emotional "traveling partners" seemed important. I was sure we would return to these topics if he decided to remain in therapy.

After thanking Frank for saying a little about himself, I essentially "restarted" the session by discussing issues regarding informed consent. According to Rooney (1992), clients who seek treatment under coercion need to discuss and understand the context of therapy in order to provide informed consent. Carefully considering these issues allows coerced clients to engage more freely in the emerging process (Rooney, 1992). Therefore, I discussed with Frank my role as a therapist, what would normally happen in a treatment setting with me, the limits of confidentiality, his right to refuse to speak or drop out of treatment at any time, and the potential consequences of this decision.

It can be difficult to discuss "housekeeping" issues without first briefly getting to know your client. This is the situation I was in with Frank. The only information I had about him was the short history he provided during our "cowboy boot" discussion and what I had learned from Richard. At the time, I still did not "know" about his drinking, the shooting, or the impending court case. All of this information came to me secondhand.

While it is appropriate to gather information about clients from referral sources, I rarely ask for too much information, beyond the presenting issue and threat or harm potential. I never begin a session with information learned from referral sources. I want to hear about the client's life from the client. In this way, the therapeutic relationship can build in a way that places me, the practitioner, in the role of learner and my client in the role of teacher and sole informant about his or her life. Our professional relationship can then build based on our unique relationship, minimizing the potential problems that come from informing a client—someone already in a vulnerable and unsure position (Glicken, 2004)—that the practitioner knows about the client's life before meeting. An additional benefit is that it limits my potential to develop preformed stereotypical "pictures" of clients based on personal biases or beliefs stemming from previous clients or my personal life-learning (Johnson, 2000).

Similarly, I rarely ask to see clinical records prior to meeting and developing a relationship with a new client. Past diagnoses, opinions, reports about previous treatments, and other material contained in most clinical records are not helpful before I know the client. The only exception is information about potential or real threats to self and others and the use of prescribed medications. The bottom line: I want to develop my own clinical impressions and professional relationship. Therefore, I encourage students and clinical trainees to avoid the temptation to begin a first session with statements such as, "So, you were sent here because of your drinking?" This type of opening question is usually a sign that the practitioner is nervous, unsure of how to proceed, or rude. Engagement works best when practitioners relax, help their clients relax, and proceed by having a "guided conversation" instead of a question-and-answer session, or worse yet, an interrogation.

Back to informed consent. Initiating this discussion without understanding the issues and context of the referral meant that I would have to revisit the issues, particularly related to the limits of confidentiality, outside reporting responsibilities, and the consequences for dropping out of treatment until I gathered more information. This was my dilemma with Frank. As our relationship grew, I would revisit these issues as I learned more about his life. For example, I could not discuss my role in his legal case or relationship with his attorney because I did not know about his legal case or attorney yet. However, I could discuss my function as therapist, the limits of confidentiality (mandated reporter issues), and the purpose of our early visits.

The Shooting and Its Immediate Aftermath

> "So, Frank . . . what brings you in today?" As an aside, be aware that even an innocuous question such as this can elicit humor. I once had an adolescent respond by saying, "My parent's car—you idiot!"
>
> "I really stepped in some shit this time," he responded, looking down at the floor. "I'm afraid I have caught a serious case."
>
> "You want to tell me about it?"
>
> "I shot my wife. I mean, I didn't kill her, just wounded her slightly in the hand. . . . I didn't mean it . . . she must have done something to startle me . . . and I was having one of those nights."

With gentle probing, Frank went on to describe the circumstances of the shooting. He said that he had been sleeping . . . having one of his "restless" nights. At some point, his wife apparently opened and shut a door in the hallway outside the bedroom. The noise startled him awake. He remembers rolling off the bed, grabbing the handgun he kept between the mattress and box spring, and shooting in the direction of the noise. Frank recalls at that moment hearing his wife yelling for him to stop shooting.

> "It's almost like I was in a trance or something," he said, fighting back tears. It was clear that this was traumatic for him, and his wife too, I'm sure. Among other things, shooting his wife challenged his earlier statement about being a proud family man.
>
> "Then what happened?"
>
> "The loud bang of the shot woke me up and I ran to her . . . I couldn't believe what I did."

Frank described his shock and horror at discovering that he shot at his wife. When he saw the wound, he immediately called for an ambulance. The police arrived at about the same time as medical help. After Fiona left for the hospital, Frank confessed to the police that he was the shooter. After allowing him to arrange for a neighbor to watch his children, the police arrested Frank for assault with a deadly weapon. At his arraignment, his wife helped convince the judge and prosecutor to set low bail, allowing Frank to return home the next day.

"What did you mean when you said you were having one of those nights?"

From the look on his face (tense) and his body language (closed while turning away from me in his chair), this was a sensitive question. "You know . . . I was restless, having dreams about things. . . ."

> "Do you mind if I ask what you mean by 'dreams about things?' I was being careful here not to push too far too fast, risking closing him down and ending what I interpreted to be the beginning of a good professional relationship.
>
> "Yea . . . I guess. Some nights I can't sleep . . . I see things from 'Nam, you know . . . I remember things and that makes me restless and jumpy. I guess that was one of those nights." He went on. "Sometimes I see those people, hear the noises, and feel like I'm back there in the bush. I don't know . . . I just gotta get over it," he said with his voice trailing off, muffled by a deep sigh of resignation to the reality of his life haunted by the demons of war.

In the aftermath of the shooting, someone called the local Child Protective Services (CPS) office to investigate Frank and Fiona's ability to protect their children. The local CPS worker, in concert with the prosecutor and the police, elected to leave the two children at home with the family. However, despite Fiona's pleadings, Frank moved out of the house into a nearby hotel immediately after the shooting. He said that he couldn't bear to look his wife in the face after what he "had done" to her. Frank said that his attorney recommended that he seek help immediately. "So, my attorney gave me that other guy's name and he sent me to you . . . That's why I'm here," Frank said.

Treatment History

"What happened when you met with Richard?"

I routinely spend time exploring clients' previous treatment experiences, trying to find clues about how to engage them in treatment. Exploring previous treatment experiences with new clients is an important part of the engagement process (Johnson, 2004). I am not as interested in dates, times, and lengths of stay as I am in clients' perception of their relationship with former practitioners, their likes and dislikes about the experience, and the clients' perception and opinion about a former practitioner's "theory" about their problems. From a carefully planned discussion, I learn valuable information about how to approach and engage clients in a therapeutic relationship that has the chance to be more successful than previous treatment attempts.

"I just didn't like that guy," Frank said. "It was nothing big, but I didn't like that he told me that I was an alcoholic and that I needed to take care of that first."

"When did he tell you this?"

"Damn . . . about half way through our first meeting . . . I didn't even know his name yet," Frank exclaimed. "I don't know why he said that. I came here cuz of the shooting . . . not cuz of my drinking."

Frank had been required to attend "drunken driving classes" on two different occasions following his arrests for drunken driving. "These were a waste of my good time," he stated. "You know, lectures about the evils of drinking, and drinking and driving . . . and those movies with all the dead bodies. Hell, they didn't bother me, not with . . ." Frank did not finish his sentence.

He described his arrests for drunken driving as a combination of "bad luck" and "no big deal." "Hell, as much as I drive, I'm bound to get caught. It's no big deal . . . It certainly doesn't mean I'm a drunk!" He went further, "I got friends that been arrested four or five times and they're not drunks . . . I guess I'm just livin' under a dark cloud."

"Is drinking something you don't want to talk about then?"

"Nah . . . we can talk about it all you want. I'm telling you that I don't have a drinking problem . . . I am not an alcoholic!"

As a practitioner trying to engage Frank in a therapeutic relationship that had only existed for about 30 minutes, his responses to the last line of questioning served as a warning. While he was willing to discuss shooting his wife, and drinking per se, he was not open to discussing the possibility of a drinking problem. This presented an interesting dilemma, one that confronts most substance abuse practitioners—their client's unwillingness to discuss substance abuse.

Simply looking at what I already knew about Frank's drinking (multiple drunken driving arrests, statements from Richard about his daily drinking, and his sensitivity toward the subject), it would have been easy to assume, based on my experience with other clients, that Frank had a serious alcohol problem. Moreover, if I were working from the disease model—the most preeminent model in the United States for working with substance abuse (Johnson, 2004)—then I would have believed that Frank should work solely on his drinking before working on any other issue. This was Richard's approach and it obviously did not work. It was clear, based on Frank's response to Richard, that I would have to take a different approach if he was going to engage in treatment. That is not to say that I am opposed to the disease model, because I am not. However, regardless of what I think, feel, or believe about his behavior, history, or treatment needs, I still did not know him. I did not know if he had a drinking problem, despite the drunken driving arrests. I suppose it was possible that he was the unluckiest fellow in the world.

Therefore, my interest, even if he had not warned me about the touchiness of the subject, was to understand his history and thoughts, feelings, and behaviors in the context of his personal multi-systemic cultural environment (Johnson, 2004) and not to assume or intimate that he had a problem with drinking, even if I thought he did. Perhaps Frank was right after all. Maybe Richard assumed he had a drinking problem based on Richard's biases and perspectives and not solely on Frank's behavior. On the other hand, perhaps Richard was correct and his timing and/or approach were off. I have always believed that it's not what you say as a practitioner that causes problems, but when and how you say it. That is, timing is everything. I had a long way to go to understand Frank, a long road between where we were at that moment and the point where it was prudent to engage in serious clinical decision making.

"Why do you think Richard thought that you were an alcoholic?"

"I don't know," Frank said in an excitable tone, "You tell me."

This was a critical moment in our relationship. How I approached this topic would determine whether a therapeutic relationship could develop between us. We had an excellent beginning, but clearly drinking was the proverbial "line in the sand" for Frank. Worse yet, I only had about 15 minutes left in our first 1-hour session. Not only did I have to proceed delicately, but I had time problems as well.

Practitioners must routinely confront and manage time and content. On the one hand, this was an excellent moment to delve into this sensitive area, primarily because he brought it up. On the other hand, should he decide to explore the subject, we did not have time to finish the exploration. There are three phases to every session: social, work, and termination (Johnson, 2004), and practitioners must manage these transitions as gracefully and seamlessly as any other part of the practice process. My decision had to be based on whether he had done enough work that day, and if not, was there time for more work before terminating the session.

"Did he ask you about your drinking?"

"Yes . . . that's all he asked about. I drink yes . . . always have, but that's not a deal I can worry about now. Shit man, I shot my wife and might be going to the joint."

"Yea . . . you could be. What do you hope coming to me can do about that possibility?"

"I don't know . . . James (his attorney) thinks that if I come to counseling it might help show the man that I'm sorry and serious about not letting this ever happen again."

"And if the man thinks that . . . ?"

"Then maybe, I won't get any time for this. I mean . . . Fiona has forgiven me . . . she understands. . . . "

"She understands what?"

"That I didn't mean to . . . that I'm not a violent man . . . I love my family . . . I've just been all confused lately. Sometimes it's worse than others."

"How long have you been confused?"

"Since the war man . . . since 'Nam,'" he said while looking away, his voice trailing off. "I don't know . . . "

"Do you think drinking is part of your confusion?"

"NO! Hell, it's about all that helps!"

By this time, the end of our session was rapidly approaching. I had to move toward terminating the session and trying to elicit his agreement to come back for a second session. In his case, and after the seriousness of the information we discussed, his return would be a positive indicator that he was engaging in treatment.

"Frank, I'd sure like to look at your confusion with you . . . if that'd be OK."

Frank nodded in apparent agreement.

"I don't know if I can help, but I can sure give it a try, if you're up for that. How about another meeting next week?"

"Alright."

With that, we ended. I thanked him for coming and for discussing his personal "business" with me, a total stranger. He sighed. I interpreted that as an acknowledgment that the session had indeed been difficult. We scheduled for the following week at the same time. He left after a handshake. What I wasn't sure if his departure was a permanent departure from treatment, or if I would see him again.

Questions

The author took a nonconfrontational approach with Frank, concerning himself more with engaging the client than with getting his entire story. Yet, many substance abuse practitioners would believe that a more direct approach is what clients with substance abuse problems need to help with their denial. This is more than simply a theoretical or style difference. The professional literature is beginning to produce a body of research that specifically addresses this difference. Therefore,

1. Explore the substance abuse and treatment literature looking for evidence of the efficacy of both a nonconfrontational approach and a confrontational approach in substance abuse practice. Develop a position based on a balanced exploration of all sides of this argument.

At the end of the first session, Frank had revealed important clues about his problems, experiences, and worldview. As you prepare for the second meeting,

1. Based on the information given in the first session, generate a list of Frank's problems and strengths.

2. What is your initial assessment? Write it down in narrative form.

3. What areas of Frank's life need further exploration in the next session, and how do you plan to approach the issues when and if he returns?

Session Two—One Week Later

I'd had a busy week by Frank's next scheduled appointment. Yet, I wondered all week whether he would return. Happily, when I walked to the small waiting area of our offices, there was Frank sitting in the corner reading a sports magazine—10 minutes early! Dressed this week in what appeared to be the same clothing as before, Frank walked into my office and found his seat.

"It's good to see you," I said.

"Yea . . . I wasn't going to come back, but my wife said I really should. So, I'm here mainly because of her."

This is another common response by coerced clients. Frank was denying the value in treatment and his role in choosing to attend by "blaming" his return on someone else. This was his way of saying "I am not ready to admit that I want to come, so I'll say I'm doing it for my wife." Yet, here he was. I chose to interpret this positively. Since I always pay more attention to actions than words, especially when working with coerced, potential substance abuse clients, Frank's return for a second visit meant that a relationship had begun. Notice I said "begun" and not "developed." I sensed that we were still a long ways from having a "developed" therapeutic relationship.

I had two primary goals for this visit. The first was to collect as much multisystemic life information as possible, hopefully focusing on his family, substance use, military service, and the shooting. The second goal was to monitor our relationship in an effort to strengthen what we had begun the week before. Therefore, the extent to which I accomplished the second goal would directly determine the extent to which I accomplished the first. Frank would determine how far we would delve into his life story. At this early stage in treatment, I was still willing to "back off," and not scare him away. There will come a time when I might confront Frank, just not this early in treatment.

"How was your week, Frank?"

"Hard, man . . . I hate that damned hotel, but I'm not ready to go home yet."

"Why not?"

"I'm ashamed . . . Fiona wants me home, but I'm still having trouble looking at her."

"What will have to happen before you're ready to go home?"

"Time, man . . . I just need some time . . . but if those idiots at the hotel keep partying all night, I might need less time that I thought," he said with a laugh. "I just gotta work some things out in my head."

"Such as . . . ?"

"You know . . . some things. Like, how could I do this and how can I face her . . . that kind of shit. I'm the kind of guy that needs to think stuff through . . . figure it out for myself before I talk about it."

Frank was sending another "stop" message. "OK, I'd be happy to talk about that stuff when you're ready," I said, pausing in such a way that made changing the subject more natural and my intentions to do so obvious. My sense of the conversation and his body language (closed and rigid) led me toward a less threatening approach. "I was hoping to learn more about you . . . your family and things like that. Sound alright with you?"

"Yea . . . sure. What do you want to know?"

The primary mechanism that I use to explore client history is a three-generation genogram and an eco-map. A genogram is a graphical way to describe a person's life and issues, in the context of his family system (Bowen, 1985) and, when combined with an eco-map, the relationship between the client, family, and community becomes clear (Hartman, 1978). While I happen to use a genogram format, there are many ways to achieve the same result. It is important for practitioners to find a style, procedure, or format that allows them to collect multi-systemic client data and proceed in a way that does not make clients feel interrogated. Often, new practitioners use agency-provided formats as a guide for history collection. Given the nature of most formats, it is easy to turn this important function into the kind of question-and-answer interrogation that I believe is counterproductive. My advice: strive to have a conversation, not an interrogation. It is difficult to build a conversation around a series of preordained and preordered questions that are often closed-ended in nature and construction.

"Let's start by talking about your family. If you don't mind, I will be drawing a picture of your family while we speak. I need pictures to remember," I said, laughing.

"Getting old is a bitch, huh?" This casual comment was important. Frank was feeling relaxed enough to joke with me. This is a good sign.

Questions

1. As we proceed through the remainder of the case, draw Frank's three-generation genogram and eco-map.

2. What is the practical value of a genogram and eco-map during assessment and treatment?

Frank's Extended Family

Frank was the second of four children born to his parents, Fred and Betty. Fred had married Betty 37 years earlier, just prior to their moving north from Mississippi in the search for work and a new start away from "the rednecks and bigots" in the south. Frank's father was a 62-year-old African American, recently retired after 40 years working the production line for a major automaker. Frank described his father as a strict disciplinarian, who demanded that his children stay out of trouble and follow orders. His father always said that the way for Blacks to survive was (is) to obey the law and keep quiet—never give the White man any reason to notice them. Of course, in Mississippi during the Depression, Whites did not need reason to go after Blacks. According to Frank, their southern heritage and links to a slave past were important in his family, mostly because of his father's constant reminders.

Frank's father took pride in his ability to support his family, often working overtime so that his family could live well. Frank's father always said, "No more sharecroppers in this family." Since his retirement, Frank said that his father had been "hanging around the house," meeting friends to play cards, and trying to enjoy life. Frank also said that his father was a lifelong drinker, "nothing serious," but that he had been drinking more since retirement. However, Frank was careful to say that his father was not an alcoholic. "He's a strong man who can handle his liquor . . . besides, after his life, he deserves to drink if he wants to."

I simply nodded, and moved on.

Betty was about to retire from her career as a public school teacher. She returned to college and earned her teaching certificate some years ago, an achievement that brought pride and a sense of accomplishment to his father. Frank described his mother as a religious woman, who was the "heart and soul" of the family. Mother was the person who insisted that the children attend church, do well in school, and demanded that all of her children graduate from college ("the best way to keep out from under the White man"). While Frank said that he loved and respected his father, his mother was the most important person in his life next to his wife. Mother brought "balance" to their lives, while father provided strictness, discipline, and a keen sense of family and cultural history.

Frank described his older sister as a person with "problems." She had been married twice and had one child from her first marriage. That marriage dissolved when the family learned that her husband was beating her. Frank described him as an alcoholic who could not control himself. He blamed her ex-husband for getting his sister into drinking and, eventually, drug use. She recently remarried but, according to Frank, the marriage was doomed. They were both heavy drinkers and drug users. He claimed that he didn't worry about her child much, because his nephew mostly lived with Frank's parents. Frank's father helped her get a job at the same plant as he, but the family was worried that she might lose her job because of her drinking and other problems. "Losing her job would send her way over the edge," Frank stated.

Frank's younger siblings (sister, 30 years old, and brother, 28 years old) were both single and worked at the auto company. He stated that both siblings were "doing well," and neither had any significant problems. The youngest brother still lived in his parent's home. Frank had friendly relationships with his younger siblings. However, he was so "pissed off" at his older sister that he couldn't speak to her. His anger, according to Frank, came from her drinking and drugs, and not taking care of her child. "We were raised better than that," he exclaimed, oblivious to his current predicament.

"It looks like (the auto company) is a family tradition. How come you didn't follow in your father's path?" I asked.

"I could of, if I wanted to. My father promised a place for me on the line and he really wanted that. But . . . that life wasn't for me. I couldn't see being trapped on that line for the rest of my life. It's good for him and the others, but not for me . . . so I joined the Army instead."

"How'd your father take that decision?"

"Not good . . . not good at all. I'm not sure we are OK yet. He's sure now that the Army and the war are why I shot Fiona. He says the demons got hold of me . . . "

"What's he mean by that?"

"You know . . . the memories and fears . . . the stuff that comes from war." Frank was almost whispering. Then, in a sudden change of attitude and affect, he uttered, "I don't want to talk about this shit . . . not now."

"OK, fine by me."

While his defensiveness was obvious, I was encouraged because he ended his statement with "not now." He did not say that he never wanted to talk about the war and its aftereffects; he just did not want to talk about it now. I would wait for the right time. It would have been a fatal mistake to push him or confront what some practitioners might interpret as denial or resistance. I hoped that we would have time to come back to the topic. Therefore, on we went discussing his family.

Fiona's Extended Family

Fiona was the eldest of two children. She was born in South Korea and moved to the United States with her parents when she was young. Her parents were "traditional" Koreans, according to Frank. That is, they believed that Fiona should have married in her race, not an American and especially not an African American. Her father owned and operated a small business in the city. He worked long hours for relatively little wage. Fiona's mother primarily cared for the family when not helping her husband in the family business, where she served as the bookkeeper.

Her parents immigrated to the United States during the Korean War and found a growing Asian community in the city comprised mainly of Korean and Chinese immigrants. In recent years, there was an influx of Vietnamese refugees moving to the area as well. According to Frank, Fiona's parents maintained their traditional values, including their language, because of the Asian enclave in the city. The family spoke Korean in their community and in Frank's presence. "That really bothers me . . . they won't even speak to me in English. I always feel like they're making fun of me."

He described both in-laws as "polite" and "quiet" people. According to Frank, his in-laws had never accepted him or Fiona's marriage to him. "They even ignore me politely!" Frank and Fiona hoped that the grandchildren would ease the tension, but it did not. While they "love" their grandchildren, they refused to speak to Frank and were constantly trying to influence Fiona to divorce him.

"What do you think is happening since the shooting?" I asked.

"Wow . . . I'm sure they're giving her some serious shit now."

"Has she said anything?"

"Nope, but she wouldn't. Fiona tries to keep this stuff away from me . . . especially now, I'm sure."

Fiona's younger sister married a Korean man five years earlier. They had one child and lived in the same community as her parents. His sister-in-law worked part-time in the family business, and his brother-in-law worked for a local computer company. While Frank claimed that Fiona's sister and husband were friendly people, there was tension. Fiona had a relationship with them, but kept it secret from her parents. "We were hoping that her sister would find a nice American man to marry . . . oh well."

Frank and Fiona

Frank met Fiona at a party shortly after returning from Vietnam. They immediately began dating and were soon engaged. They married four years later (seven years earlier), despite the problems with her extended family. In fact, her family refused to attend the wedding. Frank's father "gave" Fiona away in place of her father.

Before the children were born, Fiona worked various jobs in retail. She liked work-ing, but her heart was set on having a family. She often stayed with her sister dur-ing Frank's many overnight trucking assignments.

Frank described Fiona as a loving woman who understood him and what his life had been like since the war. "She is the only one that understands me . . . and now I go and do this." He said that she was an excellent mother, the person who held the family together when he was working or unable to be around because of his "internal partners." "She would do anything for us . . . I was really lucky to find her," he stated. "Plus," he said with a smile, "she's beautiful." He described Fiona as "Asian-looking, thin with long shiny and silky black hair . . . I love just looking at her."

Two years earlier, Fiona gave birth to their first children—twin daughters. While Frank was happy to have children, the additions caused him problems. The chaos that came with children, especially to first-time parents, intensified because they had twins. While Fiona loved the added responsibility and the "constant noise," it was especially troublesome for Frank. "I have a hard time with all the stuff that goes on . . . all the time," he stated.

"What stuff are you talking about?"

"You know . . . the noise, the crying, and the constant mess that goes with hav-ing two children all at once. It makes me nervous and edgy . . . I just want to get away from it. Sometimes, I just have to go . . . I have a hell of a hard time getting any time to relax."

He went on, clearly agitated, "I love my kids . . . they are my babies and I would do anything for them and Fiona. I mean . . . it's not them, it's me. Sometimes I can't take it."

"What do you do when it gets to you, Frank?"

"I get out of the house. Its not that I get mad . . . I don't get mad at the kids, don't hit them or anything like that. I just have to leave."

"Where do you go? Do you have friends that you see?"

"I don't have many friends . . . in fact; I don't think I have any really good friends. Since the war, I've not been the kind of guy to have buddies. I have my work, Fiona, and the kids . . . that's enough for one person. I like to be alone . . . that calms me down."

"What else do you do to relax during these times?"

"I drive, I like to drive, either my truck or my car. Fiona knows this and she never gives me any shit about it. I just need to get away for a while, and then I'm fine."

We had arrived at an important moment. The next logical question pertained to Frank's drinking. My dilemma was how to approach the subject without getting the same angry and defensive reaction as Richard. I had two choices. The most nonthreatening approach would be to ask about his drinking as part of our routine history taking, using the "cover" that I needed the information to "fill out the file." This approach allows sensitive clients permission to discuss the issue because it does not appear that the practitioner is looking for problems.

My other choice was to ask about his drinking in context, when it was the next logical question or when the discussion naturally led to the issue. This was the case with Frank. However, this was risky, especially during the second session. He either could have stopped talking altogether or participated in the conversation. This is typical of the decisions that practitioners make "on the fly," as it were. Call it intuition or a gut feeling, but there is simply no empirical data available to guide this decision. How to proceed is based on practice experience and practice wisdom. Whatever decision I made at that moment was determined by my sense of the strength of our relationship and my sense of what and how much was he willing to risk with me. Remember, this issue drove him out of treatment with Richard.

I decided to ask. "Do you ever drink some to help you relax?"

"Yea . . . sometimes I do. Having a few takes the edge off . . . that's for sure."

Whew!

Drinking and Legal History

"How long have you been drinking, Frank?"

After hesitating, he said, "Since I was 12 or so . . . had my first drinks at a family retirement party. My grandfather retired and I ran around drinking half-filled drinks left by everyone."

"How about now, do you drink regularly?"

"Yea I do. I drink something everyday. I like how it tastes, but like I said, it takes the edge off . . . makes me relax."

"Have you noticed a change in how much or how often you drink since the shooting?"

"I guess . . . I'm drinking more in the last few weeks. I don't have the kids or Fiona around . . . and I haven't been working. So, I drink . . . it helps man."

"When did you begin drinking regularly . . . how old were you?"

"Oh . . . probably 16 years old. Weekends, parties, football games . . . you know the high school shit."

"When did it become more than weekend party stuff?"

"'Nam . . . " his voice trailed off. "There wasn't much else to do over there 'cept drink and smoke weed, and God knows we did a lot of both."

"Still smoking weed (marijuana)?"

"Nope, that was one thing Fiona called a halt to. She didn't care if I drank, but no drugs . . . and I haven't."

As it turns out, Richard's original information was correct. Frank had a long history of drinking to intoxication and legal troubles stemming from his drinking. As our discussion proceeded, Frank's trepidation about discussing his drinking history subsided. My gamble paid off, but we were on relatively safe ground. I was not accusing Frank of having a drinking problem. He stated earlier that he was willing to discuss drinking, just not drinking problems. Franklin (1992) states that African American men are sensitive to labeling, that they need to feel part of the decision, including the decision about the nature and extent of their problems. That hurdle was yet to come.

Frank said he graduated from casual social drinking during high school to regular, daily, and heavy drinking in Vietnam. By the time he arrived home from the war, he was drinking about twelve bottles of beer per day, as well as a pint of liquor. Over the eleven years since his discharge, his drinking had remained at or near this average daily level. He reported regular alcoholic blackouts and feared that he would have physical withdrawal if he went without alcohol for more than one day. He experienced "the shakes" every morning, but was able to ward them off by having "a little something" in his coffee with breakfast. He also stated that he had tried to cut down several times, to no avail.

Since the shooting, Frank said that his drinking increased "quite a bit." He went on to say that on the day of sessions he drank just enough to be calm, but not enough for it to show. He would drink as soon as he left my office. His current routine was to retreat to his rented hotel room with a case of beer and a bottle of gin to drink, watch television, and "think." Frank said that he smoked marijuana daily during the war, but had not used that or any other drug since he met and married Fiona. He did not take any prescribed medication.

> "Has drinking ever caused you any troubles . . . legally, personally, on the job, stuff like that?"
>
> "Oh yea, it has. Not at home or with my family, but I seem to be somebody that gets caught drinking and driving."

Frank then told me about his three arrests for drunken driving over a ten-year period. His latest arrest happened within the past year. He was on probation for this offense when the shooting occurred. He reported never having done any jail time for his convictions, always receiving probation and drunken driving school. His attorney, a specialist in drunken driving offenses, was able to keep him out of jail and keep his driver's license current because of Frank's professional and family responsibilities. Frank could not earn a living and support his family without a driver's license.

On the day of the shooting, Frank had been drinking "hard." He spent the day in front of the television watching professional football games. He claimed that he had consumed "at least a case of beer," but that it had been a "relaxing day of football." He fell asleep early, but had been restless all night, disturbed by his dreams that night; dreams of Vietnam and the people he once knew who were now dead.

Then he heard the door slam, he startled awake, and, in a fog, shot at the noise. Unfortunately, he wasn't in Vietnam, but in his bedroom. The noise wasn't the enemy; it was his wife, coming out of the bathroom.

We were nearing the end of a very painful and tiring session, but I had one more question for Frank, one that could either make or break the remainder of our time together. I had to ask.

"Frank, have you ever wondered if your drinking was a problem?"

There was a long pause, perhaps 20 seconds. It seemed like 20 minutes. Looking down and then up directly into my eyes, he muttered, "Yea . . . I'm beginning to wonder about that."

"What makes you think that, now?"

"I don't know . . . and I'm not saying that I am an alcoholic . . . but it seems like when all the shit comes down on me, it's always when I'm drinking. I don't know."

"Can we explore that some more, say . . . next week?

"OK . . . but, what do you think? Do you think I have a problem? Am I an alcoholic?"

"Well, it's a complicated issue, and I'm not sure I'm can say one way or another right now. I need to talk to you more about it and some other things before I make that claim. It looks like, from what you have told me, that it is a possibility, but I'm not sure yet."

Frank nodded. I have always believed that chemically dependent people know they have problems, even if they do not admit it or are highly defensive about it. Denial protects the chemically dependent from admitting problems to others, not necessarily from admitting problems to themselves. If they do not admit problems publicly, they are relieved from having to take responsibility for their publicly admitted problems. Hence, I believed that Frank knew he simply could not admit it to a stranger who may have to report to the court someday. However, he knew he had a problem with alcohol, and he was getting close to admitting it.

However, I had one more topic to address. Given his history of heavy drinking and its potential to cause significant health problems (Johnson, 2004), I inquired about the last time he visited his physician for an examination. He stated that he had a physical examination about "two years ago," and that he was healthy. I asked him to schedule another physical examination, and to ask the doctor to perform blood tests and check his liver and kidney functioning to ensure that he did not have any drinking-related health problems. I offered to call his physician and let him know about the tests he needed. Frank agreed, and promptly signed a release of confidential information form that allowed this contact to occur. I also provided Frank with a pamphlet that discussed alcohol-related health risks to read later.

"How about next week we discuss this more, and, maybe, if you're ready, discuss 'Nam some."

"Alright . . . 'Nam will be tough though."

"I know . . . I've talked to others about it. That's some difficult stuff to remember."

Questions

In this session, Frank revealed much about his drinking history and how drinking affects his life, both in the present and over time. While it is still too early to make a final diagnosis, it is time to consider Frank's condition. Therefore, find a DSM-IV-TR (APA, 2000) and locate the section on substance use disorder.

1. Beginning with the criteria for substance abuse, compare Frank's information to those criteria. Does he meet the diagnostic criteria for substance abuse?

2. Then, compare his information to the criteria for substance dependence. Does he meet those criteria as well? Based on this initial finding, make your initial diagnosis of his drinking.

3. At the end of the session, Frank asked the author if he thought Frank was an alcoholic. The author did not answer him directly. What is your position on how the author handled that exchange? If you were in that place, how would you have handled that question? Defend your position with information from the practice literature, your practice experience, and through discussion with student-colleagues.

Prochaska and DiClemente (1992) and DiClemente and Prochaska (1998) elaborated the Stages of Change model that posits five stages of change, called, from the earliest to the latest: precontemplation, contemplation, action, maintenance, and relapse. I use these stages as assessment indicators of a client's level of motivation (Johnson, 2004). Based on outside readings about this model and the stages of change/motivation,

1. At the conclusion of the first session, what stage do you believe Frank was in? Defend your decision.

2. At the end of the second session, what stage was Frank in? Defend your decision.

3. If you decide that a change of stage occurred between session one and two, what were the reasons for his change?

4. What would your plan be for the next session? Why?

Third Meeting—The Turning Point

Frank returned for his third session the following week. However, this day Frank was different. He had been drinking. He said that he drank before the first two sessions also, but today I could tell. He appeared intoxicated. For the first time, I could smell alcohol on his breath and his affect and mood were elevated. He was more excitable, awake, and talkative than before. Clearly, Frank was more "social" when intoxicated. Perhaps this was the "Frank" that his family and close friends knew, instead of the serious, soft-spoken and guarded person I knew.

Why today, I wondered? Why did Frank drink before today's session and not earlier? Could it be that he was ready to reveal himself to me, or was it because of what I wanted to discuss? What I did know for sure was that this session would be interesting. However, before proceeding, I had an important decision to make. Since Frank was intoxicated, should I see him or reschedule the session?

Seeing Intoxicated Clients: A Dilemma for Practitioners

Frank's intoxication at the beginning of the session raised two important questions for practitioners. How to tell if clients are intoxicated and if so, what should they do about it? The answer to the first question is not as obvious as it may seem, while the answer to the second is controversial. Let's take them one at a time.

Recognizing Intoxication

Clients rarely show for an appointment grossly intoxicated, to the point where they are stumbling, slurring, or throwing up all over everything. I have only experienced this five or six times in more than 20 years. Moreover, while I cannot prove it empirically, those who did appear highly intoxicated usually did not have serious substance abuse problems. People with serious or chronic substance abuse problems rely on being able to "pass" without detection. They often develop a behavioral tolerance that allows them to be intoxicated while acting relatively normal, especially around people they do not know. In addition, contrary to the popular myth, most chemically dependent people can stop using drugs for an appointment or even a few days to avoid detection through urinalysis or blood testing (Johnson, 2004). Hence, knowing whether clients are under the influence during a session is not as easy as it may seem.

To answer this question, practitioners should know what intoxication looks and smells like, for a wide variety of substances. If you smell the odor of alcohol, marijuana, or heavy mints and mouthwash, this could be a cue that clients are intoxicated. If they act as if they are manic, or if after 10 to 15 minutes in the session their mood switches from agitated and energetic to sadness and lethargy, perhaps they used cocaine in the parking lot before the session. It is important for practitioners to have basic knowledge about drug effects and to recognize from actions, behaviors, smells, and other visual cues (i.e., pupil configuration, etc.) people under the influence of alcohol or other drugs (Johnson, 2004).

They Are Intoxicated—What to Do?

This is the controversial part. Many believe that practitioners should not see intoxicated clients in therapy. These practitioners routinely terminate sessions with "substance abuse clients" if they admit to having a drink that day. Yet, many of these same practitioners will meet with clients with non-substance abuse related problems, even if they admit to having just left a "three martini" business lunch. I strongly disagree with this practice and believe it is disingenuous at best and hypocritical at worst. From my perspective, intoxication is intoxication, whether people admit to having a substance abuse problem or not.

Therefore, I do not automatically cancel an appointment with an intoxicated client. This decision depends on three factors. First, can they participate in the session, or are they too intoxicated? Second, are client behaviors or attitudes so erratic that practitioners may be at-risk for an attack or some form of abuse during the session? Third, do the intoxicated clients need immediate medical attention?

If the answers to these questions indicate that clients can understand and participate, are not erratic or dangerous, and not sick, then it is acceptable and helpful to interview them, even for a few minutes. It can be an enlightening experience to interview clients when they are intoxicated to compare their intoxicated and sober presentations. This is especially true if the interview includes significant others and/or family members (Steinglass, Bennett, & Reiss, 1987). The differences can be astounding. Therefore, I say go ahead and meet with intoxicated clients, but make sure to ask about their level of intoxication directly. Do not act as if you do not know they are intoxicated, this makes you appear untrustworthy and naïve in your client's eyes.

If you choose to cancel the appointment or send them home early, do not just pack them off, especially if they drove to your office. If your intoxicated clients have an accident after leaving your office, you could be liable. Instead, offer to call a taxi (even if your agency must pay), offer bus fare, or call someone to pick them up. Moreover, if they are intoxicated and you choose to send them home, do not scold them as if they are misbehaving children. This is not the time for a lecture on why they should act more appropriately, why they are probably not suited for treatment, and how you will have to report the offense to their probation or parole officer. If you feel compelled to lecture or scold—and you should never do it—wait until you see them again and they are sober. Simply cancel the appointment, make sure to write the next appointment time down in case their memory fails, and move on to your next session. If clients push you for an explanation, simply say that you can discuss it next session.

As stated earlier, this topic is controversial and elicits strong opinion. Social workers and other professionals get angry at the thought that someone with an uncontrollable illness would have the audacity not to control it for the practitioner's benefit. Remember, treatment is for client's benefit, not ours. Our job is to make them comfortable, not vice versa.

Dealing with Frank's Intoxication

Following my own advice, I asked Frank about his drinking in my best, nonoffended voice.

> "Hey Frank, it looks to me like you've been drinking today. Is that right?"
> "Yea . . . yea, I did . . . but I'm not very drunk, I only had a few."

He was not agitated or threatening and he appeared to be coherent and ready for the session, so I proceeded. "Why did you drink today?"

> "This shit is hard, man . . . this is some serious shit we're talking about. . . ."
> "What shit?"
> "'Nam . . . 'Nam man."

Frank began to cry, in the restrained way that men often do—a cross between the need for release and fear of humiliation. Frank was, after all, a combat veteran. I'm sure that combat veterans are not used to crying. Apparently, he pondered my suggestion at the end of last week's session about the content of this session. If you remember, I suggested that we talk about Vietnam and his drinking. He was showing me that his drinking was perhaps a way to gather the courage to discuss very serious and personal issues in his life. The two issues, drinking and Vietnam were fundamentally linked in Frank's multi-systemic world.

> "What about 'Nam makes it so difficult to talk about?"
> "The shit I saw . . . what we had to do. . . ."

Frank was growing agitated, his eyes reddening from the salty sting of choked-back tears. Frank proceeded to tell me a frightening, ironic, and hauntingly tragic tale; one that could shake even the most hardened and seasoned therapist. I had heard horrible accounts of combat in Vietnam from other clients and friends, and worked with Holocaust survivors and their children as a family therapist, but this story and its connection to Frank's current dilemma was difficult to believe. He must have been making it up, or was he?

Frank recalled that his first tour of duty in Vietnam had been relatively uneventful. He spent most of his time in rear areas doing maintenance. Aside from the occasional mortar attack and other minor skirmishes, he was sheltered from combat. Thus, he chose to reenlist, figuring that his second tour would be as uneventful as the first. Besides, he did not want to go home and face the fallout between himself and his family over his joining the Army in the first place. Frank figured that one more year fixing jeeps wouldn't be that bad. However, before long, things changed.

At some point during his second tour, Frank volunteered for combat duty. Other soldiers teased and challenged him to become a "man" and fight the enemy. Under this pressure, he soon found himself in a small encampment in the jungle. Within a few days, he was on guard duty (working the point) outside the encampment. He and another soldier were the first line of defense against a surprise attack by the North Vietnamese. According to Frank, one day while on point, their position came under attack by North Vietnamese soldiers.

During the firefight, something strange occurred. A Vietnamese woman, with long dark hair, appeared in the middle of the fight. She was pushing a carriage, and in the carriage were two small children—girls, he recalled. As the woman approached their position, Frank's partner said that they would have to "deal" with her because she might be Vietcong. They knew not to trust anyone, even a woman with two children in a carriage. She might be carrying weapons or worse yet, booby-trapped with explosives. It was coming down—at least to Frank and his comrade at that moment, under fire, in the Vietnamese jungle—to a decision. It was going to be either them and their lives, or her life and the lives of her two children. They could not ignore this odd situation. What if her job was to kill them, or, what if she was simply in the wrong place at the wrong time? This was a classic example of two 19 year olds, under fire in the jungle, making life and death decisions. As Frank stated so eloquently, "we were just boys . . . how could we decide who lived and died? We just knew it wouldn't be us that died."

As Frank told this story, he began to cry. He closed his eyes, as if he was visioning this woman, an Asian woman with long dark hair with two babies, walking directly into a firefight. As he spoke, I immediately became cognizant of the connection between then and now, between the war and his family, between the Asian woman and her two children of his memory and his Asian wife and their twin daughters of his present. "Oh my goodness," I thought, trying not to change facial expression or body language, "this woman is his wife, at least in his mind's eye."

"What happened to the woman and her children?"

"We had to make a decision . . . but it wasn't that deliberate, you know. It's not as if we had a big discussion and took a vote. It was faster than that . . . you don't have time to decide in a firefight. Shit man, the gooks were swarming all around us. And here was this woman . . . where she shouldn't be."

He paused and took a deep breath, almost as if he was sucking up the courage to go on with the story. He looked me straight in the eyes,

"We cut them down . . . both of us . . . just cut them up. . . ."
"And?"

"The bag she was carrying exploded. She was coming to get us . . . to kill us along with her children and herself. She was only about 100 yards out . . . much longer and we would have been toast."

He stopped crying. He suddenly seemed clearer than before, as if he cut his emotions off from the specifics of the story. Leading to the killing, his emotions were free and flowing, but when he talked about killing, there was no obvious sorrow, no emotion, just calm and quiet words. He looked as if he were back in the war, with the focused and unemotional look of a combat veteran. He seemed to have cut himself off from his feelings about killing. Perhaps, this is how it had to be for Frank to live. Maybe this was a "normal" adaptive reaction to living through the horrors of the Vietnam War. I couldn't know for sure, I hadn't been there, walking in his combat boots. It would have been easy for me to judge him. I could not allow that to happen at this vulnerable moment in Frank's life. It is possible that I was one of the few people alive that he had ever spoken with about this incident.

I cannot say with certainty that this event happened just the way Frank described. My guess is that it did. However, social constructionism suggests that whatever actually happened that day in the jungle was not the issue. The issue for Frank was what he remembered or believed happened. His world revolved around his memory of a very specific, traumatic event that found Frank killing an Asian woman and her two children during the war. His perception of that event and its obvious connection to his life, emotional state, and more importantly, to the shooting of another Asian woman (Fiona) who also happens to have two children, became the basis for our future work. Historical accuracy took a backseat to his memory and perception of the events from so long ago.

My Dilemma

Frank's experiences in the Vietnam War exposed a personal and professional dilemma, one that I had to overcome to continue working with him. You see, I was an anti-war protester. Had I been drafted, I was off to Canada with the blessings of my family and friends. I was not going to fight President Johnson and Nixon's "war." To this day, I remain strong in my convictions against the use of military force unless as a defense against direct attack (Johnson, 2002). In this case, my political beliefs were on a collision course with Frank's life story and experiences. I had to be careful.

It is important that practitioners remain vigilant about potential conflicts between client lives and stories and their own lives and stories. The fact that we learn to be open and nonjudgmental, and that the National Association of Social Workers (NASW) Code of Professional Ethics (2000) requires as much, does not mean it automatically or necessarily occurs in practice. Our professional training does not preclude us from being human beings who live and interact in the social and political world. We each bring our personal attitudes, beliefs, and values to the interview room, creating the potential for conflict and, in its worse case, imposition of our attitudes, values, and beliefs onto the lives of our clients. Our professional responsibility as helpers requires that we develop the habit of exploring our personal beliefs, attitudes, and values to ensure that they do not come in direct or even indirect conflict with our client's beliefs, attitudes, and/or values. In other words, we must do for ourselves what we ask of our clients—address our own "stuff" on a regular basis.

How, you ask? One way is to visit a therapist, but there are alternative ways that can be just as effective. For example, addressing these issues should be a major part of routine clinical supervision. Skilled clinical supervisors often focus as much on areas of potential value conflicts as on technical clinical application. Outside formal on-the-job supervision, I recommend maintaining a group of respected peers for this purpose. I have met regularly with colleagues to discuss cases for years.

Another avenue for supervision I have used successfully involves journaling, or better yet, process recording. Keep a personal journal about your practice, focusing not on interventions, but on your feelings and attitudes about clients and your interactions with clients. Ask yourself difficult questions and respond at length. For example, do you like your clients? We each have clients we do not like. There is no shame in that, unless these feelings somehow enter the treatment room. Periodically, allow a trusted colleague to read and comment on the journal. Whatever route one chooses to use to monitor ones feelings and attitudes is not the issue. The issue is that as professionals, we must do something on a regular basis. By avoiding value conflicts, the possibility that we will impose our beliefs onto our clients lessens, freeing us to develop open, trusting relationships and pursue an empowering relationship that builds on client strengths as well as client cultural beliefs and practices.

This was my dilemma with Frank—how to continue being open to his experience outside the context of my anti-war beliefs. It took some work on my part between sessions and in consultation with colleagues. In the end, because I was aware of my issues, I could avoid any conflict during the session.

Frank's Emotional Conflict

"Frank, as you tell me this story today, how does it make you feel?"

"Oh man . . . when I think about it . . . its bad . . . I don't know how to feel about it. I did what I had to do, but look what I did . . . It was them or us . . . what could I do? I had to kill her . . . I was scared and she was trying to kill us . . . you'd have done the same thing . . . right?"

"I can't say what I would have done, since I've never been in that spot . . . it was her or you, wasn't it? It was war . . . did you have any other choice?"

"NO," he shouted, "I had no choice. The choice I made was to reenlist . . . I couldn't let her kill me or my buddy."

Frank went on to reveal his "main" emotional conflict. On the one hand, he killed a woman and her children; on the other hand, he was a soldier in war, trained and paid to kill the enemy—whoever and wherever they existed. While he seemed to understand his duty, he had struggled all of these years with the guilt associated with performing his duty. Moreover, public sentiment at the time (propagated by us protesters) did nothing to help with his guilt. In his mind, the term "baby killer" actually applied to him, and he had not resolved it in his own heart and mind. He had no venue or support to address the issues. He felt hated and despised when he returned from the war, and like most veterans at the time, he bottled his experiences and feelings inside, hoping they would go away. They did not.

We spent the remainder of the session discussing his overwhelming guilt; the intense feelings he experienced since that day in the bush and how he discovered that alcohol muted the intensity of his feelings and temporarily resolved his internal conflict. We discussed the devastating impact that the lack of public or even family support had on his adjustment to post-war life, and how there was no formal or informal means of support available to him or other Vietnam veterans after the war. He felt alone with his memories, guilt, and shame and his nightmares, alcohol, and the open road.

As the session ended, I grew concerned about Frank's safety. He no longer appeared intoxicated. I suppose that 90 minutes of this level of intensity took care of that. I had other worries. Given the intensity of the story and his feelings, his drinking, and access to weapons, I wondered about Frank's potential for suicide. By the end of the session, he seemed calm, almost peaceful. He did not appear to be a candidate for suicide. Perhaps finally telling his story began the process of lifting his burden. Yet, my professional and humanistic responsibility was to ensure, to the best of my ability, that Frank was not at-risk for suicide.

Roy (1993) offers the following factors as potential indicators of suicide risk. Evans and Farberow (1988) suggest that a clustering of these factors signals an increased risk. Below I list the factors, along with information pertaining to Frank related to each factor.

1. *Gender.* Men tend to commit suicide more often than women do; European American males are more likely than African American males to commit suicide (U.S. Bureau of Census, 1995). Frank was an African American male.

2. *Marital status.* Single/divorced/widowed adults are significantly more likely to attempt suicide than married adults. While Frank was married, he recently separated because of the shooting.

3. *Coexisting depressive disorder.* There is a strong correlation between depression and suicide (Procter & Groze, 1994). Risks increase when depressive symptoms and substance abuse combine. While his diagnoses were not firmly established, Frank exhibited symptoms that appeared depressive.

4. *Adverse life events.* An individual who has suffered an adverse life event(s) is at increased risk. Frank shot his wife, was arrested, and separated from his family. Moreover, he experienced a significant adverse life event during the war and had revisited this event during the session.

5. *Recent discharge from treatment for alcoholism.* The first four years following treatment are associated with a higher risk for suicide. Frank was just entering treatment for alcoholism, but had not quit drinking.

6. *A history of suicide attempts.* A history of suicide attempts, regardless of their intensity or lethality, is associated with an increased risk of suicide attempts in the future. During the second session, Frank denied ever having a desire to commit suicide, but things had changed since then.

When it comes to suicide risk, I ask about it directly and concretely. In Frank's case, I believed he was at-risk, since he met each criterion discussed above except the one regarding history of suicide attempts. Therefore, I needed to screen him for suicide risk that day, and in the future. He was treading through an emotional and experiential minefield and he drank. This combination could be lethal if not attended to regularly.

> "Frank, I have to ask. Given your circumstances and all, are you thinking about killing or harming yourself?"
>
> "No man . . . I have a family and kids. I'd never do that to them."
>
> "Have you ever thought about it?"
>
> "No . . . I told you that before. I love my family. After living through the war and all, I want to live. Hell, I just want things to be normal. So no, don't worry. I'll be alright."
>
> "OK. If anything ever changes, you can call here, or the people at this number (local hotline) if you can't reach me."
>
> "Cool . . ."

My concern subsided. Not only was he firm in his response, but he was looking to the future and his family as reasons for living. Had I suspected suicidal ideation, I would have assessed his responses to the following four indicators to determine the immediacy of risk (Johnson, 2004):

1. Did Frank intend to use a relatively lethal method?
2. Did he have the means available?
3. Did he have a plan in mind?
4. How specific was his plan?

The most important factor for determining the seriousness of a suicide threat is the individual's plan, with risk increasing when plans are detailed and specific.

Another indicator of seriousness occurs when a person's chosen methods are lethal and readily available (Hack, 1995). Fortunately, I did not need to worry about these indicators, at least today.

As someone who regularly treats people with alcohol problems, I had a portable breathalyzer in my office. Frank agreed to have his blood alcohol level (BAL) tested before leaving to ensure that he was able to legally drive home. His level fell far below the legal limit of that era, so he was safe to drive himself.

Frank shook my hand, heaved a big sigh, wiped his eyes, and left. Since one can ever be sure about suicide risk, I hoped that I would see him again.

Case Summary

In the preceding pages, I described Frank and his current situation in significant detail. This account of my work with Frank takes you through the first three sessions of what became a 13-month professional relationship. While Frank's case was unique because of his unusual and dramatic war experiences, how our relationship developed was not unique. That is, by focusing on rapport and engagement during the early stages of therapy instead of confrontation, intervention planning, and change, even coerced clients can progress from what some would call resistant to what I call engaged, willing partners in the therapeutic process.

From the point where Frank and I began, to the end of the third session, he had changed. No, he had not stopped drinking or resolved his issues, but he had changed. His change began when he shared his story. He was no longer in the predicament of being alone with his demons and feeling hopeless that his life will never be different. He was developing hope. He had demonstrated, by his willingness to return each week and delve into intimate personal experiences and feelings, that he had hope for his future, that his life could be different in the future. He was becoming "hooked" on possibility, instead of overwhelmed by problems and limitations. He was beginning to realize that he could be an agent for positive change in his life. The process of empowerment had begun.

However, our work is not complete—not even close. This is where you come in. It is now your task to work with Frank and his demons. As you move forward planning for the remainder of the case, do not be fooled into believing that the level of engagement and commitment Frank exhibited to this point is permanent. My experience says that it is one thing to engage clients to the point where they will relive and relate their lives. This is the "easy" part. It is a different task entirely to help Frank deepen his commitment to himself and his family and take concrete steps toward a new life. Under your care, Frank is about to confront his own dilemma of change (see earlier discussion, and Johnson, 2004). That is, Frank has choices, none of which will appear promising from his perspective at this moment in his life. It is your job as practitioners to help Frank find his way from this point forward, keeping in mind that the relationship will have to build with every step of the process, or treatment will likely fail.

This is the point in Frank's case where you take over. What happens next? I am passing Frank to you for completion. Good Luck!

Assessment, Diagnoses, and Treatment Planning

Here, your job is to develop and write a comprehensive narrative assessment of Frank's life, his family, and his environment. Your narrative assessment should reflect the multi-systemic information gleaned from Frank during his three sessions. The multi-systemic narrative assessment becomes the client's case history report (Johnson, 2004) and includes a comprehensive diagnostic statement that integrates essential client information into a coherent description of his life, history, and current circumstances. The case history report concludes with a multi-axial DSM (APA, 2000) diagnosis (or, in this case perhaps, multiple diagnoses), and/or a Person-In-Environment (PIE) score (Karls & Wandrei, 1994a, 1994b). There is a debate within social work about the pros and cons of the DSM diagnostic system that is outside the scope of this text. To review these issues, I encouraged you to look elsewhere (Johnson, 2004; Glicken, 2004; Kirk & Kutchins, 1992).

The multi-systemic case history report should lead directly to a multi-systemic and multi-modal written treatment plan (Johnson, 2004) that is understandable and agreeable to your client. This plan should include your client as a full partner in the process. This will be especially important in Frank's case, given the importance of African American males being partners in the treatment process (Franklin, 1992). There are many formats available to develop treatment plans (Johnson, 2004; Perkinson & Jongsma, 1998), use whatever format you want to enhance your learning in this case.

Questions

1. **Finish drawing the three-generation genogram that you began earlier.** Also, develop an eco-map that best represents Frank's involvement with multiple social systems and organizations in his environment.

2. **Make a list, with supporting evidence, of the main issues in Frank's life at this moment. Include in that list, a list of Frank's personal and environmental strengths that pertain to each of the issues you listed.**

3. **Develop a written multi-systemic case history report complete with diagnostic statement. Determine Frank's multi-axial (five axes and GAF scores) DSM diagnosis, or multiple diagnoses if indicated. Be sure that the information contained in the case history report clearly defends your diagnostic decisions. It is not appropriate to base diagnostic decisions on assumptions, only direct evidence provided by your client. In addition, you may apply the PIE classification system to determine Frank's level of social functioning.**

- If you were to meet with Frank, what additional information would you need to contribute to a more holistic comprehensive case history report?
- Be sure to make whatever strengths Frank may have a central part of the case history report and diagnoses.

4. Based on the case history report, develop a written treatment plan that includes short- and long-term treatment goals. Include what methods of treatment and support you will utilize.

- What treatment theory or combination of theories do you believe best fits Frank and his reality? Defend your decision.
- What theories or approaches does the latest empirical evidence in the field recommend?

Intervention Planning and Implementation

Based on the comprehensive case history report and written treatment plan developed above, it is now time to decide on intervention strategies.

Questions

Based on the treatment theory or theories chosen and defended above, list each intervention you would use in your work with Frank. Specifically, for each intervention, include the target issue, intervention and modality (i.e., group therapy) you chose, and the theoretical justification for each.

1. What other options might be available should these interventions prove ineffective?

2. What does the latest empirical evidence in the field suggest for each target issue? How does this evidence match with your intervention strategies?

3. When developing treatment approaches, do not overlook nontraditional approaches and approaches that target multiple systemic levels (i.e., individual, family, community, advocacy, etc.).

4. What factors and strategies will you use to build trust and engagement during the intervention phases of your work? How will you assist Frank as his motivation for change waxes and wanes over the coming weeks and months?

Termination, Aftercare, and Follow-Up

Preparing for termination begins early in the treatment process. Proper termination includes many factors, beside how your client progresses in treatment. Hence, this exercise will help you think about the various issues that go into successful termination, aftercare, and follow-up.

Questions

1. List and explain the general factors to consider in developing a successful aftercare plan for substance abusing clients.

2. List and explain the issues in Frank's life to consider when planning for termination and aftercare.

3. What indicators (Frank's progress in treatment) will you use to determine when it is an appropriate time for termination?

4. Plan a specific strategy for termination, aftercare, and follow-up that best fits Frank's reality and professional standards of practice. What does the latest empirical evidence in the field say about these issues?

Evaluation of Practice

Evaluation is important to the practice process. Preparing to evaluate Frank's progress in treatment must begin during the early stages of therapy. Evaluative efforts not only allow practitioners to know how their clients are progressing, areas where you need to change your approach, and when it may be appropriate to terminate treatment, but also contribute to the knowledge base of the field and profession. Additionally, most funding sources—private and public—require evidence of practice evaluation and documentation of client outcome. Therefore, developing methods for practice evaluation are essential. Here, this is your task.

Questions

1. Based on your knowledge of research and evaluation methods, develop a plan for practice evaluation that measures both practice process and client outcome.

2. Explain the rationale for your approach and how both targets (process and outcome) are integrated to give an overall evaluation of your practice efforts with Frank.

Bibliography

American Psychiatric Association (2000). *Diagnostic and statistical manual of mental disorders.* (4th ed., TR). Washington, DC: Author.
Bowen, M. (1985). *Family therapy in clinical practice.* New York: Aronson.

Cingolani, J. (1984). Social conflict perspective on work with involuntary clients. *Social Work, 29:* 442–446.

Connors, G. J., Donovan, D. M., & DiClemente, C. C. (2001). *Selecting and planning interventions: Substance abuse treatment and the stages of change.* New York: Guilford Press.

DiClemente, C. C., & Prochaska, J. O. (1998). Toward a comprehensive, transtheoretical model of change: Stages of change and addictive behaviors. In W. R. Miller & N. Heather (eds.), *Treating addictive behaviors* (2nd ed., pp. 3–24). New York: Plenum Press.

Evans, G., & Farberow, N. L. (1988). *The encyclopedia of suicide.* New York: Facts on File.

Franklin, A. J. (1992). Therapy with African American men. *Families in Society: The Journal of Contemporary Human Services,* 350–355.

Glicken, M. D. (2004). *Using the strengths perspective in social work practice.* Boston: Allyn and Bacon.

Hack, T. (1995). Suicide risk and intervention. In D. Marlin & A. Moore (eds.), *First steps in the art of intervention.* Pacific Grove, CA: Brooks/Cole.

Hartman, A. (1978). Diagrammatic assessment of family relationships. *Social Casework, 8,* 467–474.

Johnson, J. L. (2004). *Fundamentals of substance abuse practice.* Belmont, CA: Thomson-Brooks/Cole.

Johnson, J. L. (2002, Spring). Silence over Kosovo: Social work and self interest. *Reflections: Narratives of Professional Helping, 8*(2), 4–13.

Johnson, J. L. (2000). *Crossing borders—confronting history: Intercultural adjustment in a post-Cold War world.* Lanham, MD: University Press of America.

Karls, J., & Wandrei, K. (1994a). *Person-in-environment system: The PIE classification system for functioning problems.* Washington, DC: NASW.

Karls, J., & Wandrei, K. (1994b). *PIE manual: Person-in-environment system: The PIE classification system for social functioning.* Washington, DC: NASW.

Kirk, S. A., & Kutchins, H. (1992). *The selling of DSM: The rhetoric of science in psychiatry.* Beverly Hills, CA: Sage.

Miller, W. R., & Rollnick, S. (2002). *Motivational interviewing: Preparing people to change addictive behavior* (2nd ed.). New York: Guilford Press.

Mills, C. W. (1959). *The sociological imagination.* New York: Oxford University Press.

Murdach, A. D. (1980). Bargaining and persuasion with nonvoluntary clients. *Social Work, 25*(6): 458.

National Association of Social Workers (2000). *Code of Ethics of the National Association of Social Workers.* Washington, DC: Author.

Perkinson, R. R., & Jongsma, A. E., Jr. (1998). *The chemical dependence treatment planner.* New York: Wiley.

Prochaska, J. O., & DiClemente, C. C. (1992). Stages of change in the modification of problem behaviors. In M. Hersen, R. M. Eisler, & P. M. Miller (eds.), *Progress in behavior modification* (Vol. 28, pp. 183–218). Sycamore, IL: Sycamore Publishing Co.

Procter, C. D., & Groze, V. K. (1994). Risk factors for suicide among gay, lesbian, and bisexual youth. *Social Work, 39,* 504–512.

Rooney, R. H. (2002). Working with involuntary clients. In A. R. Roberts & G. J. Greene (eds.), *Social workers' desk reference* (pp. 709–716). New York: Oxford University Press.

Rooney, R. H. (1992). *Strategies for working with involuntary clients.* New York: Columbia University Press.

Roy, A. (1993). Risk factors for suicide among adult alcoholics. *Alcohol Health & Research World, 17,* 133–136.

Steinglass, P., Bennett, L. A., & Reiss, D. (1987). *The alcoholic family.* New York: Basic Books.

Thibaut, J. W., & Kelley, H. H. (1959). *The social psychology of groups.* New York: Wiley.

U.S. Bureau of the Census. (1995). *Statistical abstract of the United States: 1995* (115th ed.). Washington, DC: U.S. Government Printing Office.